THE ART OF THE SAINT JOHN'S BIBLE

A Reader's Guide to

Pentateuch, Psalms, Gospels and Acts

THE ART OF
THE SAINT JOHN'S
BIBLE

A Reader's Guide to Pentateuch, Psalms, Gospels and Acts BY SUSAN SINK

DONALD JACKSON — ARTISTIC DIRECTOR

THE SAINT JOHN'S BIBLE

Collegeville, Minnesota

The Saint John's Bible
published by
Liturgical Press
www.sjbible.org

Design by Jerry Kelly
Cover images by Donald Jackson

LIBRARY OF CONGRESS CATALOGING-IN-PUBLICATION DATA

Sink, Susan.
  The art of the Saint John's Bible / Susan Sink.
    p. cm.
  Includes bibliographical references and indexes.
  ISBN 978-0-8146-9062-8
  1. Saint John's Bible—Illustrations. 2. Illumination of books and manuscripts—Wales. 3. St. John's University (Collegeville, Minn.) I. Title.
  ND3355.5.S29S56 2007
  745.6'721--dc22   2007003564

The author gratefully acknowledges the contributions to this volume from the Committee on Illumination and Text. It could not have been written without the careful notes and educational pieces crafted by the Committee as the volumes of *The Saint John's Bible* were produced. Much of the information on individual illuminations comes directly from these pieces. Ellen Joyce generously read for accuracy on points related to illuminated manuscripts and the Middle Ages. Tim Ternes helped me get information whenever I needed it, and Carol Marrin facilitated. I also consulted and selectively used text from both *Illuminating the Word* by Christopher Calderhead, published by Liturgical Press, and the BBC video production *The Illuminator*. Of invaluable help was Father Michael Patella, OSB who read drafts and consulted on the theological interpretations and reflections that made their way into the text. I am only one reader of the Bible, and the resulting text is just one offering in the long discussion that began before Donald Jackson put quill to vellum to write the first word of the book of John, and will continue wherever the Word goes into the world.

CONTENTS

Bibliography   113

Appendices

"The continuous process of remaining open and accepting of what may reveal itself through hand and heart on a crafted page is the closest I have ever come to God."

DONALD JACKSON
from *The Illuminator*

INTRODUCTION

Illuminate: \vt\ from *in* + *luminare* to light up, from *lumin-, lumen* light. 1a: to enlighten spiritually or intellectually b: to supply or brighten with light; 2a: to make clear b: to bring to the fore; 3: to make illustrious or resplendent; 4: to decorate (as a manuscript) with gold or silver or brilliant colors or with often elaborate designs or miniature pictures.

S TRICTLY SPEAKING, there can be no illumination of a manuscript without gold. Although the definition has been expanded to apply to any brightly-colored illustration, the relationship to light is lost in this broader usage. It is gold that reflects the light to the viewer. In this way, the light is meant to come out of the illumination, not reside in it. In an illuminated Bible, the art attends to the revelation in the words. Text and image both reflect God's presence, both reveal God's mystery.

From an artistic perspective, silver has the same effect, but its use was scaled back because, unlike gold, it oxidizes black and worse, eats through the parchment. Extensive use of gold leaf, applied to the page over a surface of gesso, is often rubbed with a burnishing tool and made to shine even brighter. Gold became more common in Western manuscripts in the twelfth century, in imitation of Eastern mosaics, icons, and manuscripts. In the Eastern or Byzantine tradition, a background of gold is symbolic of heaven, the incorruptible outside of fallen creation, a tradition that has carried over to the West.

Illuminations are full of symbolism and by nature theological interpretations. Contemporary theology is exciting in part because of its openness to both the present and the past, and for its increased ecumenical sensibility. If the second half of the last millennium, from the Reformation in the sixteenth century through the twentieth century, was a period of constant schism and breaking off into multiple denominations within Christianity, the last half of the twentieth century seems to mark a shift to a new process of integration and reconciliation, as denominations share their treasures with each other and many spiritual traditions focus on their similarities rather than their differences. The ecumenical movement, as well as movements within individual traditions, has brought about greater understanding of what it means to worship one God and share the same Scriptures. Additionally, contributions from the fields of science and technology and increased connection with the global community have expanded our vision of human experience. They have also expanded our visual vocabulary to be able to embrace new symbols and contemplate new images in the context of the revelation of the Bible. These developments make possible the range of images on the pages of *The Saint John's Bible*, including the double helix of DNA, mandalas, meticulously drawn butterflies and dragonflies, and an image of the Twin Towers of the World Trade Center in New York. You will find as well a variety of images of Christ—as worker, as shaft of light, as Word, as teacher, as baptized, as transfigured, as crucified, as resurrected Lord.

The Saint John's Bible is more than an artistic work, more than a book. The project is a source of reflection, for the team that creates it and for everyone who views it either in reproduction or at exhibits traveling throughout the world. As people have looked at the images and read the text, they have become more interested in the ancient arts of calligraphy and illumination, and the way text and image work together in an illuminated Bible. To help readers deepen their understanding of the process, *The Art of The Saint John's Bible* defines terminology specific to calligraphy, and explains some of the traditional elements of illuminated manuscripts. It also includes an index that identifies the artists associated with specific works, and collects small reproductions of decorative elements and text treatments as well as the illuminations. This guide is designed as a reference book. The reproductions here are meant as references to the larger scale reproductions in the volumes of *The Saint John's Bible*. It will be difficult to see enough detail in this book alone to do a meaningful reflection.

Like all illuminated Bible manuscripts, this one reflects the spiritual aspirations of the people who created it. The Committee on Illumination and Text, comprised of biblical scholars, theologians, artists, and historians, reflected deeply and broadly on the relationship of text and art to tradition and proclamation. The calligraphers and artists brought their energy and spirit to every visual element. Donald Jackson, the lead artist, designer, and calligrapher on the project, says of calligraphy: "It's capable of picking up emotions from inside me and putting them on the page. There's an energy that comes from the soles of my feet right to the top of my head." *The Saint John's Bible* is not a mechanical rendering of archetypical images assigned to the text. It is an original manuscript, with the whole history of calligraphy and illumination as its source of reference, but also open to the contributions of contemporary theologians, artists, and craftspeople.

Each page takes seven to ten hours to write, the scribes at the scriptorium in Wales working steadily and daily at the task. Their work is a nice parallel to the Liturgy of the Hours at Saint John's Abbey, a regular practice of gathering the community together at morning, noon, and evening to recite the psalms, listen to the word, and pray. *Lectio divina*, a prayer practice common to Benedictines, is a slow and careful, meditative reading of a text. It is easy to see why monks were so often the early calligraphers and illuminators of sacred texts.

The Art of The Saint John's Bible is not meant to be the final word on any of the images, but a starting place. We have subtitled it "A Reader's Guide" and intend it as a companion piece to the traveling exhibits and the reproduction volumes. First and foremost, it has been written with a consciousness of the way text and image work together in *The Saint John's Bible* to bring people into contact with the sacred power of God's word. Unlike images in an art exhibit catalogue or book of prints, these images mean very little without the Scripture that inspired them. For this reason, we have included excerpts from the New Revised Standard Version text that corresponds to each illumination. We hope that you will read this book with a Bible or one of the reproduction volumes, and read the entire passage before diving into the essays. Unlike illustrations in a book, the miniatures are not meant to merely represent what is happening in the story. The images are here to illuminate the Word, and the Word is also necessary to illuminate the image. For that reason we invite you to approach even this reader's guide only as a way to enhance your own experience of the text and image before you. The experience will be most rich if it is your own.

The Saint John's Bible was made for twenty-first century readers. Just as readers of earlier centuries brought their own life experience to bear when looking at images in medieval and renaissance illuminated Bibles, we expect you to come to this Bible today with your rich and varied experience. Use your experiences to contemplate the stories you read; use them to read the images you see. This reader's guide is not meant to explain or even fully open the illuminations for the reader. It is a guide, just that, to open up a few of the details, and hopefully provoke an even more rich exploration of what you read and see in the pages.

Because it is the Bible that we're exploring, the guide will take some time in the introductions and throughout to introduce the context behind the artwork. What is the Pentateuch? Why are there four gospels? Why did the Committee on Illumination and Text choose these passages to illuminate? All of this will help readers make sense of the Bible project as a whole.

When approaching the essay for each major illumination, please take some time with the Scripture passage first. At the beginning of each essay we have provided a question for you to consider. The essay gives information on the context in which the image was developed and some of the primary elements. Finally, return to the Scripture passage. What strikes you about it now you didn't notice before? Ask yourself: Have I also been "illuminated"?

PENTATEUCH

THE PENTATEUCH is a name for the first five books of the Old Testament. In their final form, they were collected from multiple sources after the Assyrian and Babylonian captivity which lasted from the first deportations in 722 B.C.E. and ended with the return in 538 B.C.E. By the time of exile, Israel had lived through its early formation, from the call of Abraham out of the land of Ur (present-day Iraq) on the way to the Promised Land. After the long period of slavery in Egypt, Moses and then Joshua led the Israelites to Canaan, where the Lord delivered a large territory into their hands.

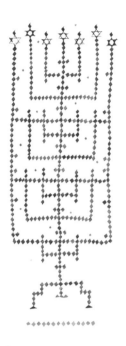

Genesis and Exodus, the first two books of the Pentateuch, tell the stories of the people of Israel from their creation stories in Genesis through the arrival at the Promised Land. In fact, after the opening accounts of creation, the flood, and other foundational stories, Genesis 18–50 tells the story of Abraham and his descendants through Joseph, and ends in Egypt. Exodus begins with the birth of Moses and takes the story right to the edge of the land which God showed him. It is here Israel becomes a nation.

By the end of the period of judges and kings, including the famous King David, the twelve tribes of Israel had become two kingdoms, Israel and Judah, and these kingdoms finally fell to Assyrian and Babylonian invaders, respectively. The captivity ended when Babylonia became part of the Persian Empire under King Cyrus in 538 B.C.E. He sent all captive peoples in his empire back to their lands and even encouraged the restoration of local religious traditions (since temples made good places for monitoring citizens and collecting taxes). It was the experience of exile and return that transformed Israel from a tribe (or set of tribes) and a nation into a people identified by religion. The displacement and inculturation of generations in exile had ruptured their identity, and now they needed a unified temple practice and text—the Torah, the Law of Moses—to unite them as the Jewish people.

They turned to the Torah, the law God gave to Moses, which is also the Hebrew name for the Pentateuch. From the time of Moses on, the

Old Testament historians tell of the relationship between the people and God through faithfulness or unfaithfulness to the Torah. When King Josiah is brought the book of the Law after a long period of unfaithful kings, he weeps and mourns, knowing that Israel has broken the covenant and so will face destruction. Tradition has long claimed that Moses himself wrote the complete Torah as given to him by God on Mt. Sinai, and that the people of Israel carried it in the Ark of the Covenant into the Promised Land. It is much more likely that most of the document we now read was written after the Israelites settled in one place, namely Canaan, and supplemented with other texts after the Babylonian captivity. In any event, it is the story of the people and their relationship to the one true God. It was written to remind them of their ancestors and of the story of God's faithfulness and promises to them—often despite their own unfaithfulness.

These are the stories meant to bring a people home to themselves, and keep them on a path with their God. The stories of the Pentateuch have indeed brought comfort to captives and to those living in oppression. Jesus quoted these texts, and in fact declared that he came not to replace the Law but to fulfill it. These books provided inspirational text for the songs and sermons of the Civil Rights Movement and other non-violent movements worldwide. A text treatment in Leviticus highlights the teaching: "The alien who resides with you shall be to you as the citizen among you; you shall love the alien as yourself, for you were aliens in the land of Egypt: I am the Lord your God" (Lev 19:34). This text has special resonance today, as countries wrestle with issues of immigration and nationalism.

The five books of the Pentateuch bring together a variety of foundational accounts and texts that underlie the Jewish, Christian, and Islamic faiths. They include the great moral code engraved by God onto tablets atop Mount Zion, the Ten Commandments. They include the two stories of creation—one of the world and humankind in seven days, the other of the humans Adam and Eve and the Garden of Eden—our first stories about who God is, God's relationship to the universe and, specifically, to humankind.

The challenges for an artist in visually representing even one of these texts are immense. On the pages of *Pentateuch*, Donald Jackson and his team have created eight illuminations that range from a quarter-page to the two-page treatment of Abraham and Sarah. Additionally, there are

THE ART OF THE SAINT JOHN'S BIBLE

six special text treatments, and a number of decorations in the margins. Whatever their size on the page, illuminations in books were also called "miniatures" in the medieval tradition. Just as the term illumination comes from the use of gold, miniature originally referred to the red ink used on manuscripts (made from minium, a type of red lead). Since the eighteenth century, however, it has been used to describe their size. You will find both terms used in this text. The following pages provide a discussion of many of these elements, together with their biblical context, as a way of deepening your experience with the art of *The Saint John's Bible*.

CREATION

THE ART OF THE SAINT JOHN'S BIBLE

What does this image say to you about the nature of creation?

Looking at the illumination, you'll notice right away that it has seven panels for the seven days. The first panel contains "fractals," the jagged geometric shapes that resemble jigsaw puzzle pieces. Fractals play a role in various collages in the Bible. They reflect glimpses, fleeting moments of clarity, and layers of symbolic meaning—not unlike our experience seeing God in Scripture.

This image, created by Donald Jackson with contributions from nature illustrator Chris Tomlin, emphasizes the tension between order and disorder, structure and chaos, even the fields of mathematics and science. What happens when we combine ideas of science and creation? Can they go together into a unified whole? Jackson suggests that the Genesis story, a story of seven days, nevertheless tells us about timelessness. It tells us about the beginning of space and time. So he assembled seven panels here, irregular and exploding from the dark primordial void, a state expressed verbally at the bottom of the first day with the Hebrew words *tohu wabohu*—formless and void.

Where do you begin on this image? What captures your eye? There's a lot of gold, and you'll see gold leaf throughout *The Saint John's Bible*, most often used to represent the presence of the divine. Gold here is symbolic of God's intervention in the chaos and his ordering of the universe and its elements. Whenever you see gold in an illumination, contemplate what it means that God is present at that moment in the story—in what way? Accomplishing what purpose? How clearly do we perceive God in the story's action?

Day one is struck through with a thin ribbon of gold. This corresponds to verse 3, "Let there be light!" In what way are God and light connected, even beyond the story of creation?

Day three is made from satellite photos of the Ganges Delta. Notice the variety of color and the sense of movement not just in this panel but everywhere.

Representing archetypal humanity, like representing

Creation

GENESIS 1:1–2:4A
In the beginning when God created the heavens and the earth . . . (1:1)

God, is always tricky. For the creation of human beings on the sixth day, Jackson used images from aboriginal rock paintings in Australia. The huntress on top is from an even earlier rock painting found in Africa. Woven in is a fragment of Chris Tomlin's coral snake, which appears more clearly in the next miniature, the Garden of Eden, which also depicts the ancient huntress, and again in the portrayal of Adam and Eve. This is all one story, and the image of creation includes elements that can carry us all the way from Genesis 1 to Revelation. The fish stamp used for the fifth day of creation, for example, was also used in the Loaves and Fishes illumination for Mark 6:30-44 and 8:1-10.

Smudged into the surface is the image of a black bird. Donald Jackson says "birds are these magical, mobile, extra-terrestrial creatures." Perhaps this bird connects the heavens and the earth, captures the movement expressed in every part of the illumination, is a creature of all realms: land, sky, and sea. "The raven is a messenger in the Bible," says Jackson. There will be birds bringing messages to Noah on the ark. A raven brought God's message to St. Benedict, patron of the Benedictine monks at Saint John's Abbey who commissioned this work.

The design of this Bible pays special attention to Benedictine spirituality, and includes images of the flora and fauna of the Minnesota landscape, as well as of the Welsh countryside where it was written in Donald Jackson's scriptorium. This rootedness in the present day and local landscape is another link between this illuminated Bible and those made hundreds of years ago. Sometimes one finds in the elaborately decorated initials and margins of manuscripts a depiction of the abbey or grounds where it was being made. Sometimes even the faces of specific monks would make their way into the paintings.

◀ Re-read the story of creation now and notice God's activity, the abundance and energy of the language, and the serenity of the seventh day. What else do you see? What is prominent? How does the illumination open the text for you?

THE ART OF THE SAINT JOHN'S BIBLE

How do these images match up to your vision of the Garden of Eden and Adam and Eve?

These two illuminations are directly related to the second story of creation in Genesis, the story of the Garden of Eden and Adam and Eve. Notice how gold is used as a frame of God's creation (including the snake). Creation is abundant, fertile, breaking the bounds of the rectangular image. Creation is messy. The beautiful but predatory harlequin shrimp, the coral snake, and several poisonous insects foreshadow the end of innocence. Adam and Eve have painted faces, also reflective of our "divided but connected relationship" with each other and with our environment.

The figures, inspired by photographs of the Karo tribe of the Omo River in southwest Ethiopia, reflect current archaeological and anthropological theories that humankind evolved from our predecessors in Africa. What other ways do the images reflect that we are made in God's image? What else do they reflect about the first man and first woman, given dominion over the earth? What do the framing images, from textiles and a Peruvian feather cape, say about humans as creators, our fruitfulness?

In the Garden of Eden illumination, the cave paintings tell of the human need to tell stories even from earliest time. Creation is a story of dominion and celebration. Adam and Eve's painted faces, along with the decorated, colorful cloth, speak of humanity's desire to rejoice in being alive. People make patterns, like the textile patterns and the curved piece of a mandala at the center left of the Garden of Eden miniature.

The mandala is an archetypal image common to many faith traditions, a word that can be loosely translated as "circle." Hildegard von Bingen saw mandala shapes in the visions she received from God, and the mandala can be seen throughout Christian architecture, in decorated dome ceilings, in the rose windows of Chartres. "The Buddhist mandala . . . is about the birth of intellect," according to Donald Jackson.

Garden of Eden & Adam and Eve

GENESIS 2:4b-25
And the Lord God planted a garden in Eden, in the east; and there he put the man whom he had formed. (2:8)

GARDEN OF EDEN

The two stories of creation in Genesis 1–2 both culminate in the place of humankind among the creatures. We are made in the image and likeness of the Creator, combining physical beauty and reason, and with the breath of life breathed into our nostrils by God (Gen 2:7). The wholeness and expressiveness of this origin is brought together in the mandala image. However, the coral snake is also here as fragments of a circle, hinting at a dark element within free will and human reason. Look for this shape in other Old and New Testament illuminations, including the opening image in the Gospel of Matthew and the page of Jesus' miracles in the Gospel of Luke.

Finally, text plays a large part in these images as well. In the margins are two quotations from letters written by the apostle Paul, tying the Old and New Testaments together. Donald Jackson saw these as captions for the pictures. The text to the Garden of Eden captures creation as alpha and omega, the beginning waiting for the final revelation. "For the creation waits with eager longing for the revealing of the children of God" (Rom 8:19). There's a sense of creative expectation: what will we be when we finish our ongoing life of grace and God's final kingdom is revealed? The passage for Adam and Eve draws our attention to the platinum background behind Eve, which acts as a mirror. "And all of us, with unveiled faces, seeing the glory of the Lord as though reflected in a mirror, are being transformed into the same image from one degree of glory to another" (2 Cor 3:18). As we move closer to Christ we will see a single image reflecting back: unified in our godliness and vibrant in the variety of our smiles. "God is within us when we look into the mirror," Jackson said of the image. "Eve and Adam are mirrors of us."

◀ What do you think the world might look like in its perfected state?

ADAM AND EVE

THE ART OF THE SAINT JOHN'S BIBLE

בראשית

GENESIS

IN THE BEGINNING WHEN GOD CREATED THE HEAVENS AND THE EARTH, THE EARTH WAS A FORMLESS VOID & DARKNESS COVERED THE FACE OF THE DEEP, WHILE A WIND FROM GOD SWEPT OVER THE FACE OF THE WATERS. ³THEN GOD SAID, "LET THERE BE LIGHT"; AND THERE WAS LIGHT. ⁴AND GOD SAW THAT THE LIGHT WAS GOOD; AND GOD SEPARATED THE LIGHT FROM THE DARKNESS. ⁵GOD CALLED THE LIGHT DAY, AND THE DARKNESS HE CALLED NIGHT. AND THERE WAS EVENING AND THERE WAS MORNING, THE ⁶FIRST DAY. AND GOD SAID, "LET THERE BE A DOME IN THE MIDST OF THE WATERS, AND LET IT SEPARATE THE WATERS FROM THE WATERS." ⁷ SO GOD MADE THE DOME & SEPARATED THE WATERS THAT WERE UNDER THE DOME FROM THE WATERS THAT WERE ABOVE THE DOME. AND IT WAS SO. ⁸GOD CALLED THE DOME SKY. AND THERE WAS EVENING & THERE WAS MORNING, ⁹THE SECOND DAY. AND GOD SAID, "LET THE WATERS UNDER THE SKY BE GATHERED TOGETHER INTO ONE PLACE, AND LET THE DRY LAND APPEAR." AND IT WAS SO. ¹⁰GOD CALLED THE DRY LAND EARTH, AND THE WATERS THAT WERE GATHERED TOGETHER HE CALLED SEAS. AND GOD SAW THAT IT WAS GOOD. ¹¹THEN GOD SAID, "LET THE EARTH PUT FORTH VEGETATION: PLANTS YIELDING SEED, AND FRUIT TREES OF EVERY KIND ON EARTH THAT BEAR FRUIT WITH THE SEED IN IT." AND IT WAS SO. ¹² THE EARTH BROUGHT FORTH VEGETATION: PLANTS YIELDING SEED OF EVERY KIND, AND TREES OF EVERY KIND BEARING FRUIT WITH THE SEED IN IT. AND GOD SAW THAT IT WAS GOOD. ¹³AND THERE WAS EVENING AND THERE WAS MORNING, THE ¹⁴THIRD DAY. AND GOD SAID, "LET THERE BE LIGHTS IN THE DOME OF THE SKY TO SEPARATE THE DAY FROM THE NIGHT; AND LET THEM BE FOR SIGNS AND FOR SEASONS AND FOR DAYS AND YEARS, ¹⁵AND LET THEM BE LIGHTS IN THE DOME OF THE SKY TO GIVE LIGHT UPON THE EARTH." AND IT WAS SO. ¹⁶ GOD MADE THE TWO GREAT LIGHTS~ THE GREATER LIGHT TO RULE THE DAY AND THE LESSER LIGHT TO RULE THE NIGHT~ AND THE STARS. ¹⁷ GOD SET THEM IN THE DOME OF THE SKY TO GIVE LIGHT UPON THE EARTH, ¹⁸ TO RULE OVER THE DAY AND OVER THE NIGHT, AND TO SEPARATE THE LIGHT FROM THE DARKNESS. AND GOD SAW THAT IT WAS GOOD. ¹⁹ AND THERE WAS EVENING AND THERE WAS MORNING, THE FOURTH DAY. ²⁰ AND GOD SAID, "LET THE WATERS BRING FORTH SWARMS OF LIVING CREATURES, AND LET BIRDS FLY ABOVE THE EARTH ACROSS THE DOME OF THE SKY." ²¹ SO GOD CREATED EVERY LIVING CREATURE THAT MOVES, OF EVERY KIND, WITH WHICH THE WATERS SWARM, AND EVERY WINGED BIRD OF EVERY KIND. AND GOD SAW THAT IT WAS GOOD. ²²GOD BLESSED THEM, SAYING, "BE FRUITFUL AND MULTIPLY AND FILL THE WATERS IN THE SEAS, AND LET BIRDS MULTIPLY ON THE EARTH." ²³ AND THERE WAS EVENING AND THERE WAS MORNING, THE FIFTH ²⁴ DAY. AND GOD SAID, "LET THE EARTH BRING FORTH LIVING CREATURES OF EVERY KIND: CATTLE AND CREEPING THINGS & WILD ANIMALS OF THE EARTH OF EVERY KIND." AND IT WAS SO. ²⁵GOD MADE THE WILD ANIMALS OF THE EARTH OF EVERY KIND, AND THE CATTLE OF EVERY KIND, AND EVERYTHING

THE GREAT SEA MONSTERS AND

ᵃ Or when God began to create or In the beginning God created
ᵇ Or while the spirit of God or while a mighty wind
ᶜ Heb adam
ᵈ Syr: Mtk and over all the earth
ᵉ Heb waters
ᶠ Heb Seas

Abraham and Sarah

GENESIS 15:1-7 AND 17:1-22
"Look toward heaven and count the stars. . . So shall your descendants be." (15:5)

ABRAHAM AND SARAH

What does this illumination tell you about the two passages in Genesis?

The covenant God makes with Abraham is at the heart of both the Jewish and Christian traditions. The monotheistic lineage of Judaism, Christianity, and Islam begins with our common father, the patriarch Abraham. The menorah, a seven-branched candlestick used in Jewish worship, is the central image of this illumination, and foreshadows the frontispiece of the Gospel of Matthew, the genealogy of

Jesus through the line of Abraham and Sarah. The menorah is thus used as a family tree, a version of the tree of life in the Garden of Eden. Do you see the leaves on this tree?

Other important elements in the story of God's covenant with Abraham are also represented. The stars fill the sky, as well as delicate gold stamped figures of arabesques or mandalas. These same stamps will be used in other illuminations, for example, at the birth of Christ in Luke's frontispiece, at the miracle of the loaves and fishes in Mark, and at the Great Commission in Acts 28. This image will connect the text to the creation and life of the church, whose origins are also here in Abraham. *The Saint John's Bible* uses recurring images and motifs to show the unity and interplay between the books of the Bible.

The menorah here is rooted in the two names, Abraham and Sarah, and rises to the inscription of the names of the children of Jacob. This is the beginning of the tree that will rise in the Gospel of Matthew to the birth of Jesus. As a parallel of that image, this family tree reminds Christians that the covenant between God and Abraham through Sarah is the root of both Judaism and Christianity.

❦ At the lower right is a black and grey figure, representing the sacrificial ram that takes the place of Isaac. Sacrifice is an essential part of the larger story, too. What else do you see of the story? In the passage from chapter 17, God instructs Abraham about the role of circumcision, and talks to him about Ishmael. Do these pieces of the story make their way into the illumination?

In what way do the butterflies and angels illuminate Jacob's vision for you?

This illumination captures an instance of God's contact with humans in the Old Testament. In two key stories, this and the wrestling with God of Genesis 32, God makes his covenant with Jacob, who is renamed Israel. It is another step in the covenant made with Abraham, and you'll remember that the menorahs in our last illumination featured the names of the twelve tribes of Israel, Jacob's sons. Here gold angels ascend and descend the space with the ladder connecting this world and heaven. The angels don't need the ladder, as they seem to circle around and through it.

Chris Tomlin's butterflies, portrayed here in accurately rendered wing fragments, are a striking presence. Butterflies, like birds, are special creatures, and seem to bridge both heaven and earth. They are often hard to keep in our vision, as their wings fold closed and they become a sliver on a leaf or flower, or as they dip and disappear into the tall grass.

❡ What does this raucous combination of elements say to you of the nature of visions and dreams, of God waking up Jacob to his promise? And what do you make of Jacob's response, that blue figure at the bottom of the page before the awesome display by God?

Jacob's Ladder

GENESIS 28:10-22
And he dreamed that there was a ladder set up on the earth, the top of it reaching to heaven; and the angels of God were ascending and descending on it. (28:12)

JACOB'S LADDER

Jacob's Second Dream

GENESIS 32:24-32
Jacob was left alone; and a man wrestled with him until daybreak. (32:24)

Where is the "story" in this miniature?

Again Jacob and God meet in the night. After reading the story of Jacob wrestling with the man, consider the illumination. It reprises several elements from Jacob's ladder, including the butterfly wings, the blue figures, and scattered gold. Unlike the earlier gold imprint, which was made by applying acrylic to crocheted textiles, the gold here is like squares and diamonds of confetti. There is another shadow figure, the moon of creation or something else. The Hebrew words are Jacob's two names, Israel in gold to replace Jacob in black. Again, the encounter between the heavenly and human world is emphasized in color and form.

But also, look back to the original illumination of creation. There is something of the chaos of the first day in these two illuminations of Jacob. What is the relationship between the two stories and their images? What is the role of chaos here?

and whatever you say to me I will give. ¹²Put the marriage present and gift as high as you like, and I will give whatever you ask me; only give me the
¹³ girl to be my wife." ▌ The sons of Jacob answered Shechem & his father Hamor deceitfully, because he had defiled their sister Dinah.¹⁴ They said to them, "we cannot do this thing, to give our sister to one who is uncircumcised, for that would be a disgrace to us. ¹⁵ Only on this condition will we consent to you: that you will become as we are and every male among you be circumcised.¹⁶ Then we will give our daughters to you, and we will take your daughters for ourselves, and we will live among you and become one people.¹⁷ But if you will not listen to us and be circumcised, then we will take
¹⁸ our daughter and be gone." ▌ Their words pleased

JACOB'S SECOND DREAM

THE ART OF THE SAINT JOHN'S BIBLE

Five passages are incorporated into this single illumination by artist Thomas Ingmire. In addition to the Ten Commandments themselves, what other elements of Israel's story do you recognize?

The Ten Commandments

EXODUS 20:1-26
Then God spoke all these words . . . (20:1)

Across the top panel four stories are represented: the burning bush, the first Passover, the Red Sea crossing, and the twelve pillars erected at the foot of Mount Sinai to represent the twelve tribes of Israel. Although the illumination is divided into panels, the events combine to make one story— the story of Israel's liberation and establishment as a nation. Look for elements: water, altar, mountain, across the top half of the illumination.

The Ten Commandments, the foundation on which these stories are built, is envisioned as a creation story. It is the creation of the moral universe, the gift of the Law bringing order to the chaos of human affairs. Do you see elements carried over from the first illumination of creation? Notice the birds—wing and eye. The familiar words of the commandments, stenciled in Stone Sans typeface as though engraved on tablets, eat through the colored background. God speaks in gold capitals here, announcing: "Here I am. I am the God of your Father. I am the Lord your God."

THE TEN COMMANDMENTS

Thomas Ingmire commented on how strange it was that God wrote down the commandments for a culture of people who couldn't read. It established the idea of God as Word, which is carried into the Gospel of John. Ingmire also did the illumination of the "I AM" passages in John's Gospel, metaphors which build directly on this declaration. Christians believe the same God revealed in Jesus Christ gave the commandments to Moses. What does it mean for God to be proclaimed in word, when God's name cannot be uttered as word, when no image can capture God?

❧ What does the jumble and jockeying of text on image say about us? What does it say about God? What is our relationship to this new creation, the law meant to restore order and harmony to the world? What is our relationship to God as Word?

This is a good place to stop and look at some of the elements besides the major illuminations. We'll look here at two: corrections and text treatments.

Corrections

In the margin on the second page of Leviticus 19, there is a little bird. The rope in its talons attach to a box of text, and its beak points to the place where the text should be inserted. This is a human mark on the project. At this place the calligrapher missed two lines in the copying. As with medieval manuscripts, the investment in labor and in vellum and ink could not be wasted. There was no crumpling up of the page and tossing it in a wastebasket when an error was made. The solution, then as now, was to make the correction an element of the artwork. Like tapestries into which a flaw is woven to show the work is not perfect, this Bible is not a product of a calculating machine, but the work of human hands.

Text Treatments

It's important to read not just the text that is extracted and emphasized, but the whole chapter in Leviticus. The makers of *The Saint John's Bible* used the special treatment of key verses to draw our attention to something in the long, didactic book of the law that is Leviticus. Let's face it. We're much more familiar with the stories of Creation, Abraham, and Jacob than with the Law of Moses for which these books get the name Torah, the Hebrew word for law. However, this law expresses God's purpose for creation and contains key tenants of our faith.

In the treatment for Leviticus 19, we see the words Jesus quoted when asked by the Pharisees in Matthew 22 to name the greatest commandment: Love your neighbor as yourself. We will also find, at Deuteronomy 6, a text treatment of the first part of Jesus' answer: "You shall love the Lord your God with all your heart. . . " (v. 5).

As we read the chapter in its entirety, we see again and again the emphasis on the poor—we are told not to pick our

BUT·THE·LORD·SAID·
TO·MOSES·&·AARON·
BECAUSE·YOU·DID·NOT·
·TRUST·IN·ME·
·TO·SHOW·MY·HOLINESS·
BEFORE·THE·EYES·
·OF·THE·ISRAELITES·
·THEREFORE·
·YOU·SHALL·
·NOT·BRING·
·THIS·ASSEMBLY·
·INTO·THE·LAND·
·THAT·I·HAVE·
·GIVEN·THEM.

NUMBERS 20:12

vineyard clean or harvest to the edge of the field, but to leave the gleanings for the hungry to pick up. It is not so difficult to see past the culturally specific references here and apply these words to our own life and times. Christianity is rooted in Judaism, and here we see that relationship in the commandment to love the Lord and neighbor and to serve the poor.

These text treatments stop us as we're flipping through the Bible. When we slow down and pay attention to the passages, we see the connections in the ongoing story. God made his covenant. God gave his commandments. God instructs the people through Moses with a law that gives more specific direction on how to live and yet is contained in the Ten Commandments.

There are nineteen text treatments in the three volumes of *The Saint John's Bible* covered by this reader's guide. An index of artists and the passages they illuminated can be found at the end.

Special text treatments form a thread to draw attention to the unfolding story of God with us, not just at the familiar stories we know and love, but deep in the books of Leviticus, Numbers, and Deuteronomy.

Before we go ahead to the death of Moses, we make a stop at Numbers 20, at the waters of Meribah, where God tells Moses and Aaron: "You did not trust in me" and names the consequence, "You shall not bring this assembly into the land that I have given them" (v. 12).

Next, in Deuteronomy 6, Israel is commanded: "You shall love the Lord your God with all your heart, and with all your soul, and with all your might" (v. 5).

Finally, in Deuteronomy 30, God finishes his declaration of the Law, saying "I have set before you life and death, blessings and curses. Choose life so that you and your descendants may live, loving the Lord your God, obeying him, and holding fast to him" (30:19-20). The law is completed here in a text treatment using the Stone Sans script

THE ART OF THE SAINT JOHN'S BIBLE

that was used in the illumination of the Ten Commandments, impressed on the page as on our hearts. Pause
awhile to read the close of Deuteronomy, where God
speaks of the importance of the Law, and where Moses
takes leave of the people.

❧ Look at the text treatments in *Gospels and Acts*. Why do
you think these particular passages have been chosen? How
do they connect to the passages chosen for special treatment in *Pentateuch*? How do they connect to Psalm 1 and
Psalm 150, the only text treatments in *Psalms*? We will return to these subjects later.

DEUTERONOMY 30:19–20

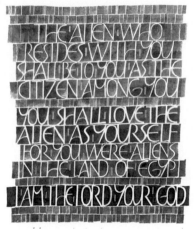

LEVITICUS 19:34

21

turning aside to the right hand or to the left until
18 we have passed through your territory." ▌ But Edom
said to him, "You shall not pass through, or we will
come out with the sword against you." 19 The Israelites said to him, "We will stay on the highway; and
if we drink of your water, we and our livestock, then
we will pay for it. It is only a small matter; just let
us pass through on foot." 20 But he said, "You shall
not pass through." And Edom came out against them
with a large force, heavily armed. 21 Thus Edom re-
fused to give Israel passage through their territory;
22 so Israel turned away from them. ▌ They set out from
Kadesh, and the Israelites, the whole congregation,
came to Mount Hor. 23 Then the LORD said to Moses
and Aaron at Mount Hor, on the border of the land
of Edom, 24 "Let Aaron be gathered to his people. For
he shall not enter the land that I have given to the
Israelites, because you rebelled against my command
at the waters of Meribah. 25 Take Aaron & his son
Eleazar, and bring them up Mount Hor; 26 strip Aaron
of his vestments, and put them on his son Eleazar.
But Aaron shall be gathered to his people, and shall
die there." 27 Moses did as the LORD had commanded;
they went up Mount Hor in the sight of the whole
congregation. 28 Moses stripped Aaron of his vestments, and put them on his son Eleazar; and Aaron
died there on the top of the mountain. Moses and
Eleazar came down from the mountain. 29 When all
the congregation saw that Aaron had died, all the
house of Israel mourned for Aaron thirty days.

f Heb lacks to his people
g Heb Destruction
h Or Sea of Reeds
i Or fiery; Heb seraphim
j Or fiery; Heb seraph
k Gk Heb which is in

When the Canaanite, the king of Arad,
who lived in the Negeb, heard that Israel was coming by the way of Atharim,
he fought against Israel & took some of them captive.
2 Then Israel made a vow to the LORD & said, "If you
will indeed give this people into our hands, then we will
utterly destroy their towns." 3 The LORD listened to
the voice of Israel, and handed over the Canaanites;
and they utterly destroyed them and their towns;
so the place was called Hormah. ▌ From Mount Hor
they set out by the way to the Red Sea, to go around
the land of Edom; but the people became impatient
on the way. 5 The people spoke against God & against
Moses, "Why have you brought us up out of Egypt
to die in the wilderness? For there is no food and no
water, and we detest this miserable food." 6 Then the
LORD sent poisonous serpents among the people,
and they bit the people, so that many Israelites died.
7 The people came to Moses & said, "We have sinned
by speaking against the LORD and against you; pray
to the LORD to take away the serpents from us." So

MAKE A POISONOUS SERPENT AND SET IT ON A POLE

AND EVERYONE WHO IS BITTEN SHALL LOOK AT IT AND LIVE

Moses prayed for the people. 8 And the LORD said
to Moses, "Make a poisonous serpent, and set it on
a pole; and everyone who is bitten shall look at it &
live." 9 So Moses made a serpent of bronze, and put
it upon a pole; and whenever a serpent bit someone,
that person would look at the serpent of bronze &
10 live. ▌ The Israelites set out, and camped in Oboth.
11 They set out from Oboth, and camped at Iye-abarim,
in the wilderness bordering Moab toward the sun-
rise. 12 From there they set out; and camped in the
Wadi Zered. 13 From there they set out; and camped
on the other side of the Arnon, in the wilderness

A POISONOUS SERPENT

What does this illumination tell us about God's punishment and God's mercy?

This miniature is part of the larger story of Moses and Aaron's faltering faith and the punishment they receive. Numbers 20 tells this story, and includes an even louder round of grumbling by the Israelites wandering in the desert than we find in chapter 21. Even after their needs are met when God brings water out of the rock, it doesn't take long for the Israelites to lose heart again. So far the illuminations have told us the story of creation, and of God's covenants and promises. They have been celebratory—even the small decoration for the story of the flood in Genesis 8 occurs when "God remembered Noah," and the waters abated (v. 1).

Here we encounter that other vision of God associated with the Old Testament. His judgment against Aaron and Moses seems extraordinarily harsh. Now when the people grumble, miserable and hungry in the desert, the Lord sends poisonous snakes which further compound their misery. However, when Moses prays, God sends the cure. But the cure is also a snake.

In Christian tradition this story has been seen as foreshadowing Christ's death and resurrection. In John 3:14-15, Jesus is quoted as saying, "And just as Moses lifted up the serpent in the wilderness, so must the Son of Man be lifted up, that whoever believes in him may have eternal life." This image reflects the theological position that the curse of the fall in Genesis (through Adam) becomes the blessing of salvation in the death and resurrection (through Christ).

There is no snake on a pole here, no realistic picture to accompany the text. This broken image reflects the broken world. God and the serpent are present not only in the colors and the geometry of creation and the fall but also in the rising toward resurrection. Thomas Ingmire created this illumination, as well as the Sermon on the Mount in Matthew and the I AM Sayings in John. Is there any way that this image also looks forward to those representations of Christ? What else do you see that is common to Ingmire's miniatures?

A Poisonous Serpent

NUMBERS 21:1-9
Then the Lord sent poisonous serpents among the people . . . (21:6)

The Death of Moses

DEUTERONOMY 34:1-12
This is the land of which I swore to Abraham, to Isaac, and to Jacob . . . I have let you see it with your eyes, but you shall not cross over there.
(34:4)

What emotions are expressed in this painting?

The journey through the illuminations in *Pentateuch* ends at Deuteronomy 34 with the death of Moses. You have seen these elements before, the rich colors used to depict the Promised Land, the colors and the quality of the brush strokes seen in earlier illuminations for Noah, for Abraham, for the stories of Israel's passage out of Egypt. Still there is separation, the dual quality that goes back to Adam and Eve, the black night of Jacob surrounding Moses who can only look but not enter the Promised Land. After Adam and Eve, Moses is our first realistically represented face, painted by artist Aidan Hart, who works as a traditional Greek Orthodox icon painter. Moses carries the tablets of the Ten Commandments. He does not enter the Promised Land, but God is with him in the filaments of gold that pierce the darkness, in the thin band that encircles his head.

This image captures the deep pain of exile that is part of the experience of early Israelites in Egypt and the first readers of the Pentateuch in exile in Babylon. It is an exile that belongs to all descendants of those banished from the garden. Moses' face registers the trials of the journey, the hope, the astonishment of seeing that which was promised. The story of Israel's release from bondage and passage to the Promised Land has had great power throughout history. It spoke to early colonists arriving in the new world of America, to slaves seeking freedom in the northern United States, to immigrants landing on Ellis Island or in San Francisco, and it speaks to people today risking their lives to cross the El Grande River. Finally, it speaks to all of us as we await our entry into God's kingdom. What does it mean that this volume ends with this image?

All year the Jewish people read the Torah in Hebrew. On a day in late October, the feast of Simchat Torah, they finish this passage in Deuteronomy, roll up the Torah scroll, and begin again immediately at the first verse of Genesis. We can also do this with *The Saint John's Bible*. Return to Genesis 1 and the illumination of creation. What do you see now

THE ART OF THE SAINT JOHN'S BIBLE

that you didn't before? Are those filaments of gold around Moses similar to the filament announcing the arrival of light in verse 3?

❧ Do you have a better understanding of our story with God? Where did we start this journey, where have we come, and what do we have before us?

Rejoice, Zebulun, in your going out;
  and Issachar, in your tents.
They call peoples to the mountain;
  there they offer the right sacrifices;
  for they suck the affluence of the seas
  and the hidden treasures of the sand.

And of Gad he said:
  Blessed be the enlargement of Gad!
  Gad lives like a lion;
  he tears at arm and scalp.
He chose the best for himself,
  for there a commander's allotment was reserved;
  he came at the head of the people;
  he executed the justice of the LORD,
  and his ordinances for Israel.

And of Dan he said:
  Dan is a lion's whelp
  that leaps forth from Bashan.

And of Naphtali he said:
  O Naphtali, sated with favor,
  full of the blessing of the LORD,
  possess the west and the south.

And of Asher he said:
  Most blessed of sons be Asher;
  may he be the favorite of his brothers,
  and may he dip his foot in oil.
Your bars are iron and bronze;
  and as your days, so is your strength.

There is none like God, O Jeshurun,
  who rides through the heavens to your help,
  majestic through the skies.
He subdues the ancient gods,
  shatters the forces of old;
  he drove out the enemy before you,
  and said, "Destroy!"
So Israel lives in safety,
  untroubled is Jacob's abode
  in a land of grain and wine,
  where the heavens drop down dew.
Happy are you, O Israel! Who is like you,
  a people saved by the LORD,
  the shield of your help,
  and the sword of your triumph!
  your enemies shall come fawning to you,
  and you shall tread on their backs.

I HAVE LET YOU SEE IT WITH YOUR EYES BUT YOU SHALL NOT CROSS OVER THERE

THEN MOSES THE SERVANT OF THE LORD DIED THERE IN THE LAND OF MOAB AT THE LORD'S COMMAND

THE DEATH OF MOSES

PSALMS FRONTISPIECE

THE ART OF THE SAINT JOHN'S BIBLE

PSALMS

WHEN THE VOLUME of *Psalms* was issued, many people asked, "Where are the pictures?" During discussions about how to render *Psalms*, the first and most important understanding shared by the team was that the book of Psalms is a prayer book. Throughout the centuries psalms have been sung and chanted by those in relationship with God. The psalms have been a way that people have approached God, and sought deeper understanding of their relationship to the divine. As such, the desire of Donald Jackson and the Committee on Illumination and Text was for a text that was as open as possible for use in the prayer life of those who turned to it. The intention was for the script to sing on the lips and in the hearts of those who read them.

Introduction to Psalms

Psalms is a liturgical book used by Christians and Jews for thousands of years. Liturgy comes from the Greek for "work of the people," and refers to various forms of public worship, usually structured around song and text. Judaism and Christianity share many of the same liturgical texts from the Old Testament, but with different theological emphases. For example, consider Psalm 23. Christians have long layered this text with John 10:11: "I am the good shepherd. The good shepherd lays down his life for the sheep." Obviously, this connection with Jesus is not a Jewish association.

Think of how the psalm resonates in light of the Israelites' wanderings in the desert and arrival in the Promised Land, or their return from the Babylonian exile. In Christian liturgies, Psalm 23 has been used in funerals, with its association of "the valley of the shadow of death" and everlasting life. This Christian theology of death and resurrection may echo differently in other religious traditions. Psalm 23 is still used in Jewish funerals and memorial services for its emphasis on comfort and trust in God.

The psalms were collected during the time of judges and kings, during the Babylonian exile, and after the return and rebuilding of Israel. In addition to songs written during this period (most famously the psalms attributed to David), the book of Psalms collected even earlier songs from the time of wandering in the desert with Moses. They were organized into five books (actually scrolls), and used by the people when they gathered at the temple to remember and reaffirm their experience of God.

The book of Psalms, however, is not a random collection of songs. The interpretation that guides this volume of *The Saint John's Bible* was offered by Irene Nowell, OSB, an Old Testament scholar and a member of the Committee on Illumination and Text. She asserts the psalms make up a book that is organized and tells a story, the same story as the history books and the prophets of the Old Testament, the story of God's faithfulness and Israel's journey into nationhood, although it tells the story in song.

Because it is not a historical book, to tie the images in the psalms to a specific historical period would be to diminish the vitality and life of the text. According to Nowell, "In the biblical worldview, to remember is to make present." The psalms do not simply collect stories of God's faithfulness in the past. Just as they did for the people gathered to sing them at the temple, they remind us of our history with God, the covenant and call to follow God's commands today. Monastic communities that have chanted these psalms in daily prayer called the Divine Office experience the beauty of the cycle of lament and praise, exile and return, pilgrimage and nationhood, wisdom and knowledge. The psalms are meant to be read prayerfully, slowly and meditatively, but also liturgically, that is in public worship. The abstract images found in the *Psalms* volume of *The Saint John's Bible* lead the mind to a greater appreciation of the complexity and grandeur of God.

The Text

The text here, as throughout *The Saint John's Bible*, is from the New Revised Standard Version (NRSV). You will notice that many of the psalms include rubrics. Rubrics are instructions for how the assembly or the leaders are to carry out the liturgy. For example, the rubric at Psalm 4 reads, "To the leader: with stringed instruments," and for Psalm 5: "To the leader: for the flutes." Both are identified also as psalms written by David. As in the other volumes, any verses that appear in the Rule of Benedict are marked with a small black cross in the margin, and with the NRSV notes on the text.

The word "Selah" is occasionally written in the right margin. The word appears in *Psalms* seventy-one times in thirty-nine of the psalms.

The origin of this word is unclear, and its meaning cannot be determined exactly. Most scholars think it is used in the Bible like "Amen." It probably comes from the Hebrew word *"calah"* meaning "to hang," as in to weigh something by hanging it on a scale in comparison to another item. *Calah* is translated elsewhere in the Bible as "measure," usually related to measuring something's value. Selah, then, is thought to be a call for the reader to pay special attention, "take measure" of the passage to which it refers.

Donald Jackson and the Committee on Illumination and Text agreed that the design and text needed to reflect the five-book structure of the Psalms. Each book was assigned a color, which was used in the headings and initial caps, and for the "Amen, Amen" that closes each book. Even more significantly, each book is written in its own script. The five books of Psalms were split between three calligraphers: Brian Simpson for Book I (Pss 1–41), Sally Mae Joseph for Book II (Pss 42–72) and Book V (Pss 107–150), with Jackson writing Book III and Book IV (Pss 73–106) and doing the text treatment for Psalm 1 and the frontispiece illuminations.

The average reader might have difficulty seeing the differences between the scripts. However, for the calligraphers it was a welcome challenge and change. A close look reveals differences in such things as spacing, slant of the letters, and roundness. Joseph and Jackson, who did two books apiece, devised separate scripts for each book they wrote, so that all five books would be unique. In the end, *Psalms* perhaps draws more attention to the art of calligraphy than any of the other volumes. Calligraphy, Donald Jackson has said, is a form "that makes you look like you really mean what you're saying." It makes the words sing—which is what the book of Psalms is all about.

Ornamentation and Frontispieces

Still, *Psalms* is not without ornamentation. Because the psalms are so closely related to chant and song, Donald Jackson started with the question, "How can we represent song in image?" The decision was made to use oscilloscopic voiceprints of the monks of Saint John's Abbey chanting at prayer. The voiceprint is represented horizontally on the page with gold bars that ground the image and tie it to musical notation. The chant of the monks flows throughout the psalm text. Look at Psalms 23–27, where the songs of David burst with gold chant.

Psalm 1

Happy are those
who do not follow the advice of the wicked,
or take the path that sinners tread,
or sit in the seat of scoffers;
2 but their delight is in the law of the LORD,
and on his law they meditate day and night.
3 They are like trees
planted by streams of water,
which yield their fruit in its season,
and their leaves do not wither.
In all that they do, they prosper.

4 The wicked are not so,
but are like chaff that the wind drives away.
5 Therefore the wicked will not stand
in the judgment,
nor sinners in the congregation
of the righteous;
6 for the LORD watches over the way
of the righteous,
but the way of the wicked will perish.

*a Cn: Meaning of Heb of verses 11b and 12a is uncertain
b Syr: Heb kiss
v Wisdom
vii Royal
1 Lament*

VII Psalm 2

Why do the nations conspire,
and the peoples plot in vain?
2 The kings of the earth set themselves,
and the rulers take counsel together,
against the LORD and his anointed, saying,
3 "Let us burst their bonds asunder,
and cast their cords from us."

4 He who sits in the heavens laughs;
the LORD has them in derision.
5 Then he will speak to them in his wrath,
and terrify them in his fury, saying,
6 "I have set my king on Zion, my holy hill."

7 I will tell of the decree of the LORD:
He said to me, "You are my son;
today I have begotten you.
8 Ask of me, and I will make the nations
your heritage,
and the ends of the earth your possession.
9 You shall break them with a rod of iron,
and dash them in pieces like
a potter's vessel."

10 Now therefore, O kings, be wise;
be warned, O rulers of the earth.
11 Serve the LORD with fear,
with trembling 12 kiss his feet,
or he will be angry, and you will perish
in the way;
for his wrath is quickly kindled.

Happy are all who take refuge in him.

Psalm 3

*A Psalm of David,
when he fled from his son Absalom.*

O LORD, how many are my foes!
Many are rising against me;
2 many are saying to me,
"There is no help for you in God."   Selah

3 But you, O LORD, are a shield around me,
my glory, and the one who lifts up my head.
4 I cry aloud to the LORD,
and he answers me from his holy hill.   Selah

5 I lie down and sleep;
I wake again, for the LORD sustains me.
6 I am not afraid of ten thousands of people

Help, O Lord, for there is no longer
    anyone who is godly;
    the faithful have disappeared
    from humankind.
2 They utter lies to each other;
    with flattering lips and a double
    heart they speak.

3 May the Lord cut off all flattering
    the tongue that makes great boast

Book I Brian Simpson

The mighty one, God the LORD,
    speaks and summons the earth
    from the rising of the sun to its se
2 Out of Zion, the perfection of beau1
    God shines forth.

3 Our God comes and does not keep si
    before him is a devouring fire,
    and a mighty tempest all around
4 He calls to the heavens above

Book II Sally Mae Joseph

On the holy mount stands the city he fo1
2   the LORD loves the gates of Zion
    more than all the dwellings of Jacol
3 Glorious things are spoken of you,
    O city of God.

4 Among those who know me I mention
    Rahab and Babylon;
    Philistia too, and Tyre, with Ethio1
    "This one was born there," they say.

Book III Donald Jackson

O LORD, you God of vengeance,
    you God of vengeance, shine forth
2 Rise up, O judge of the earth;
    give to the proud what they dese1
3 O LORD, how long shall the wicke
    how long shall the wicked exult 1

4 They pour out their arrogant word
    all the evildoers boast.
5 They crush your people, O LORD.

Book IV Donald Jackson

I was glad when they said to me,
    "Let us go to the house of the LORD
2 Our feet are standing
    within your gates, O Jerusalem.

3 Jerusalem – built as a city
    that is bound firmly together.
4 To it the tribes go up,
    the tribes of the LORD,
    as was decreed for Israel,

Book V Sally Mae Joseph

A selection of passages from the psalms, showing
the work of different scribes.
The headings for all the psalms were written by
Brian Simpson. A different color is used for each
book.

The major illumination for *Psalms* is found on the two-page frontispiece before Psalm 1. Here you see how the five volumes, set up like open scrolls, also come together to make the third of the menorahs in these volumes. The first illumination for the entire project was Donald Jackson's menorah for the Genealogy of Jesus, the frontispiece for the book of Matthew. Second, he made the menorah family tree we've already read about in Genesis, Abraham and Sarah. This third piece draws our attention again to the wholeness of the story, the shared traditions.

Additionally, the five book structure of Psalms imitates the five books of the Pentateuch. The open scrolls were used again at the beginning of each of the five books of Psalms. Donald layered them to create an image with one open scroll for Book I, two for Book II, three for Book III, and so on. Again, the vertical panels reflect the layout of the page in columns, but also the fractals of the illumination of The Creation.

FROM PSALM 89

Another recurrent motif on these pages is the stamped gold archways. In this context they speak to both the temple of Jerusalem where people first met to sing these songs, and contemporary places of worship. Our visions of chant tend to be very grand. When we hear the word "chant," we're most likely to think of a religious community in robes or habits singing Gregorian chant as they solemnly process down a long aisle or fill the choir stalls of a Gothic cathedral in Europe. This is the way we've seen chant represented in books, movies, and even television commercials. On high quality recordings, professional voices in unison echo off the stone walls. The reality is that liturgical chant today does not happen in cathedrals, but most often in

THE ART OF THE SAINT JOHN'S BIBLE

small communities that meet regularly to intone or chant the psalms as part of their daily prayer life. The stamped archways, however, also act as symbols of the way song can usher us into the presence of God.

The Five Books

Psalms 1 and 150 stand as bookends to the collection. They are independent of the five-book structure, but still thematically connected to the books in which they appear. To note their importance, they receive special treatment. The first psalm appears in its entirety in the frontispiece of the volume and is repeated at the beginning of Book I. The psalm introduces a book that is primarily laments, although all the laments end on a note of hope for the righteous. Psalm 1 lays out the terms and consequences of the covenant: "Happy are those . . . [whose] delight is in the law of the Lord," and at the end, "The Lord watches over the way of the righteous, but the way of the wicked will perish" (Ps 1:1, 2, 6).

Book II ends with a messianic psalm (Psalm 72). Messianic psalms are part of the theology that defines Jesus as the Christ, and sees him as descended from the royal line of King David. "Messiah" from Hebrew and "Christ" from Greek both mean "anointed one." In Book 2, the monarchy is seen in a very positive light, although the actual monarchy of that time was a mixed bag of faithful and corrupt kings. Books I and II probably formed the original Psalter, the songbook of David's kingdom. They seem to have been written during the time David's line was in power, the tenth to sixth century B.C.E. Most of the

BOOK IV: FRONTISPIECE

psalms in Books I and II have notes indicating they belong in the David collection. There is even a note at the end of Psalm 72: "The prayers of David son of Jesse are ended."

Books III and IV probably belong to the period right before the Babylonian exile (before the sixth century B.C.E.) and the time of the return from exile. Book III ends with another messianic psalm (Psalm 89), which begins with a very positive statement of God's promise that David's dynasty will last forever, but ends with the cry: "Lord, where is your steadfast love of old, which by your faithfulness you swore to David?" (Ps 89:49). The psalmist claims God's promise, even though the promise seems all but crushed by Israel's unfaithfulness.

Book IV begins with the only psalm attributed to Moses (Psalm 90): "Lord, you have been our dwelling place in all generations" (v. 1). The people have returned to restore the faith and the nation of Israel. By the end of the book, lament has turned to praise, and the psalmist exclaims, "Praise the Lord! O give thanks to the Lord, for he is good; for his steadfast love endures forever" (106:1). The first three books ended "Amen, Amen" but the last two end with "Praise the Lord!" Book V is a book of thanksgiving and praise by the restored people of Israel. The temple is rebuilt and the promise of a dynasty is heard again. This book explodes with praise in Psalms 146–150, which reflects both the gratitude of a liberated and restored people, and the tone of their liturgies in the new temple as they recommitted themselves to the covenant with God.

Psalm 150 has been set as a song many times. It is a glorious conclusion to the psalter. Psalm 150 was written in gold by Sally Mae Joseph. The choice of gold was related to the text treatment for the Magnificat, Mary's hymn of praise in the first chapter of Luke. Jackson saw a similarity between the two hymns, and suggested to Joseph that she tie them together visually by using the same script and burnished gold on gesso but not putting it on a background of color. In the end, the Psalms had established themselves as text on vellum, and to background one was to remove it too dramatically from the whole.

THE ART OF THE SAINT JOHN'S BIBLE

Voiceprints

The constructions that begin each of the five books of Psalms introduce other elements to the monk's chants. They are shaped like open scrolls, although the elements, like song, float out beyond the borders. They are richly layered, as though you look deeply into them. The squares are characteristic of early notation for Gregorian chant, called "neumes." Squares stacked on a four-line staff mark ascending notes, while diamonds reading left to right show descending notes. This kind of notation is still used by many monastic communities. The interplay between the vertical and horizontal reappears in the chant voiceprints that are the dominant element here.

In addition to the gold filigree voiceprints of the Benedictines, there are multicolor representations of other chant traditions also made by two computer programs that translate sound to visual prints, resembling the wave patterns on an oscilloscope in one instance, and rubbings or technical data in another. The Benedictine chant of the monks of Saint John's Abbey runs horizontally, and vertically are chants from the Jewish, Native American, Taoist, Hindu Bhajan, Greek Orthodox, Muslim, and Buddhist Tantric traditions. People have commented that they look like a cardiogram, a welcome association. Music is sometimes used to calm an erratic heartbeat, and is intimately tied to the rhythms of the heart, which are of course the rhythms of life itself.

The representations of other chant are included here below. Notice what they say about the nature of the voice or voices. The evenness of the Taoist chant is in strong contrast to the long tones followed by shifts in the Jewish and Native American chant. The close harmonies of the Greek Orthodox chant are easy to imagine.

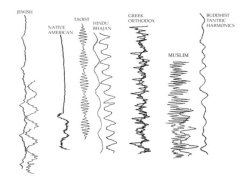

BOOK V: FRONTISPIECE

Finally, this presentation of the psalms inspires the reader to put images with the poetry of the text. The frontispiece includes the complete text of Psalm 1, a good example of the imagery in the book of Psalms. Those that follow God's commands "are like trees planted by streams of water, which yield their fruit in its season" (Ps 1:3). The wicked, however, "are like chaff that the wind drives away . . . [They] will not stand in the judgment" (Ps 1:4-5). Elsewhere you will find people compared to "the grass on the housetops that withers before it grows up," and the colorful claim, "The plowers plowed on my back; they made their furrows long" (Ps 129:6, 3). The poetry brings to our mind's eye the thatched roof and the painful marks of the whip. In the final analysis, for *Psalms*, the poetry is enough. The images exist in the minds and hearts of the community that prays and sings them. The focus in this volume, therefore, is on the calligraphy, the art that is the lifeblood of *The Saint John's Bible*.

GOSPELS

THE FOUR GOSPELS give us four distinct views of Jesus and his ministry. They were written by followers of Jesus who had their own voices and literary techniques, and who wrote for specific audiences, for liturgical use in specific communities that had their own traditions. Each gospel has its own focus and character. For example, only Matthew and Luke tell the story of Christ's birth. Whereas the Gospel of Mark focuses on Jesus' ministry, John's Gospel most often uses highly metaphorical language, as when Jesus identifies himself as the light of the world, the bread of life, living water, the gate, and the true vine. Always when we read and contemplate the New Testament, our goal is not to assemble the historical details of Jesus' biography, but to gain a deeper understanding of God with us, Emmanuel, his divinity and humanity, and the wonderful promise fulfilled by his death and resurrection.

The gospels and their accounts have inspired artists for centuries. There are great traditions of Byzantine icons, medieval illuminations, and renaissance paintings that reflect the sensibilities of believers in various places and times. An illuminated New Testament that hopes to speak to contemporary readers has even more to draw upon in terms of the history of the book and Christian art.

The Roman Catholic Lectionary, the course of readings used by Catholics during liturgies throughout the year, emphasizes the importance of each gospel. The church spends most of the year (except for Advent, Lent, the Easter season, and special feast days) reading accounts from a single gospel. In a three year cycle, the church reads primarily texts from Matthew (Year A), Mark (Year B), and then Luke (Year C). John's unique gospel, full of metaphor and with its detailed accounts of Christ's passion and resurrection, is read primarily during the forty days of Lent and fifty days of Easter each year. This lectionary, developed in the 1960s after the Second Vatican Council, with the participation of Godfrey Diekmann, OSB, a monk from Saint John's Abbey, also became the model for new lectionaries developed by Protestant denominations. The Revised Common Lectionary, used by at least twenty-five Protestant denominations in North America, came out of this ecumenical

THE GOSPEL ACCORDING TO MATTHEW

1 AN ACCOUNT OF THE GENEALOGY OF JESUS THE MESSIAH, THE SON OF DAVID, THE SON OF ABRAHAM.

2 ■ ABRAHAM WAS THE FATHER OF ISAAC, AND ISAAC THE FATHER OF JACOB, AND JACOB THE FATHER OF JUDAH AND HIS BROTHERS, 3 AND JUDAH THE FATHER OF PEREZ AND ZERAH BY TAMAR, AND PEREZ THE FATHER OF HEZRON, AND HEZRON THE FATHER OF ARAM, 4 AND ARAM THE FATHER OF AMINADAB, AND AMINADAB THE FATHER OF NAHSHON, AND NAHSHON THE FATHER OF SALMON, 5 AND SALMON THE FATHER OF BOAZ BY RAHAB, AND BOAZ THE FATHER OF OBED BY RUTH, AND OBED THE FATHER OF JESSE, 6 & JESSE THE FATHER OF KING DAVID. AND DAVID WAS THE FATHER OF SOLOMON BY THE WIFE OF URIAH; 7 AND SOLOMON THE FATHER OF REHOBOAM, & REHOBOAM THE FATHER OF ABIJAH, AND ABIJAH THE FATHER OF ASAPH, 8 AND ASAPH THE FATHER OF JEHOSHAPHAT, AND JEHOSHAPHAT THE FATHER OF JORAM, AND JORAM THE FATHER OF UZZIAH, 9 AND UZZIAH THE FATHER OF JOTHAM, AND JOTHAM THE FATHER OF AHAZ, AND AHAZ THE FATHER OF HEZEKIAH, 10 AND HEZEKIAH THE FATHER OF MANASSEH, AND MANASSEH

THE FATHER OF AMOS, AND AMOS THE FATHER OF JOSIAH, 11 AND JOSIAH THE FATHER OF JECHONIAH & HIS BROTHERS, AT THE TIME OF THE DEPORTATION TO BABYLON. 12 ■ AND AFTER THE DEPORTATION TO BABYLON: JECHONIAH WAS THE FATHER OF SALATHIEL, AND SALATHIEL THE FATHER OF ZERUBBABEL, 13 AND ZERUBBABEL THE FATHER OF ABIUD, AND ABIUD THE FATHER OF ELIAKIM, AND ELIAKIM THE FATHER OF AZOR, 14 AND AZOR THE FATHER OF ZADOK, AND ZADOK THE FATHER OF ACHIM, AND ACHIM THE FATHER OF ELIUD, 15 AND ELIUD THE FATHER OF ELEAZAR, AND ELEAZAR THE FATHER OF MATTHAN, AND MATTHAN THE FATHER OF JACOB, 16 AND JACOB THE FATHER OF JOSEPH THE HUSBAND OF MARY, OF WHOM JESUS WAS BORN, WHO IS CALLED THE MESSIAH. 17 ■ SO ALL THE GENERATIONS FROM ABRAHAM TO DAVID ARE FOURTEEN GENERATIONS; AND FROM DAVID TO THE DEPORTATION TO BABYLON, FOURTEEN GENERATIONS; AND FROM THE DEPORTATION TO BABYLON TO THE MESSIAH, FOURTEEN GENERATIONS.

process in 1992. Many of the illuminations in this volume correspond to key texts from Sunday gospel readings.

Gospels and Acts was the first volume of *The Saint John's Bible* to be completed at Donald Jackson's scriptorium in Wales. As such, it in fact established some of the visual elements and motifs that we've already seen in *Pentateuch* and *Psalms*. Because this is a Christian Bible, it understands both the Old and New Testament as the story of Jesus Christ revealed as the salvation of humanity. For that reason, and because of the richness of the tradition of gospel illumination, this volume is heavy with significant illuminations.

Again, we invite you to take your time with both text and image as you use this guide, reading the full Scripture passage before the essay for each illumination. Also remember that nothing here is definitive or exhaustive. As we exhibit pages from *The Saint John's Bible* around the country, people share insights and make connections we had not considered before. It is our hope that as you spend time with *Gospels and Acts*, you will be attentive to more than the biographical lives of Jesus and the apostles. We hope that you will read with open eyes, ears, and heart, allowing the Holy Spirit to speak as you contemplate the Word.

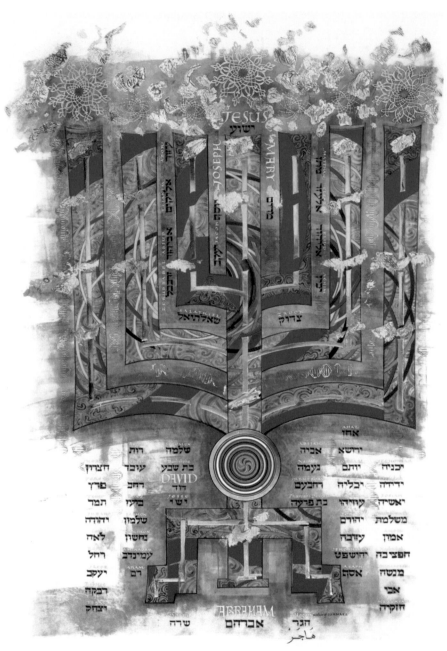

GENEALOGY OF CHRIST

THE ART OF THE SAINT JOHN'S BIBLE

What elements from previous illuminations do you see here? Why do you think they're included?

The place that each gospel begins is important. Each gospel is an account of Jesus, his life and ministry, written for use in a particular church. Only Matthew and Luke start with Jesus' birth, and they emphasize different pieces of the story. Only Matthew starts with the genealogy, and that is where we begin our tour of the New Testament illuminations.

This full-page illumination was the first Donald Jackson made for *The Saint John's Bible* project. It was done before many of the decisions about the Bible were made, before the script was even finalized. In that way, perhaps, Jackson had the most free rein with this illumination. He has said his ultimate aim was to suggest "the connectedness of all seekers of enlightenment." He did this by including symbols from several traditions. The image also draws us to reflect on life, on creation, on history and redemption, on identity.

The menorah from Jewish tradition becomes a family tree, from which the names of the genealogy branch out. Matthew wrote for a Jewish audience and set Jesus' birth within a Jewish context. The line of Jesus through David was important for establishing his divinity. Abraham and Sarah are the root of this tree, and Hagar is there too, with her name in Arabic as well as Hebrew and English, the branch that leads through Ishmael to Islam. The gilded stamps used in the center of the illustration come from illuminations of the Koran. A mandala is incorporated into the base of the menorah, again a sign of cosmic unity and wholeness found in many religious traditions.

The illumination is not just linear, rising vertically in a straight line to Jesus. Behind the menorah/tree are swirling bands of color over turbulent, churning water. Again creation is with us, as God brings order from the chaos of the human and natural world. We see this churning water again in Matthew 8:23-28, when Jesus calms the storm.

Even more striking than these abstract elements are the

Genealogy of Christ

MATTHEW 1 *An account of the genealogy of Jesus the Messiah, the son of David, the son of Abraham. (1:1)*

stamps of a double helix. With its spiral shape, it is reminiscent of many things, perhaps even Jacob's ladder from Genesis. The contemporary symbol of identity fixed by DNA ties the Bible to the twenty-first century reader and emphasizes the incarnation, the humanity of Jesus.

❧ What does this illumination say about the identity of Jesus?

THE ART OF THE SAINT JOHN'S BIBLE

What can you make out from the text on the right side of the image?

The illumination chosen for the Sermon on the Mount is the text of the Beatitudes. The complete text for the Sermon on the Mount is Matthew 5:1–7:24. In these chapters are many of the core teachings of Jesus, including the Lord's Prayer at Matthew 6:9-13. This prayer is done in a special text treatment, and elaborate initial capitals for chapters 5–8 are linked to the color scheme of the illumination and text treatment.

The illumination of the Beatitudes is by Thomas Ingmire, who also did the illumination for the Ten Commandments (Exodus 20). The gospel writer sees a parallel between Moses going up Mount Sinai to receive the Law and Jesus going up the mountain to deliver a "new law." What parallels, and what differences, do you see between the illumination of the Ten Commandments and this one for the Beatitudes? How does this jumble of the word "blessed" match or contrast with the text of the Commandments? Jesus said he came to fulfill the Old Testament Law, not abolish it. Do the two pieces illustrate this relationship?

The Beatitudes have special resonance with the Rule of Benedict and are themes for the monastic life. One motto of the Benedictines is "Pax," and their vows center on the values of simplicity, hospitality, and prayer. Some say the colors and shapes of the text remind them of the stained glass windows at Saint John's Abbey Church.

❡ What is the nature of this new law, this litany of "Blessed be"?

Sermon on the Mount

MATTHEW 5:1-12
When Jesus saw the crowds, he went up the mountain . . . Then he began to speak, and taught them, saying . . . (5:1-2)

THE BEATITUDES

CALMING OF THE STORM

³⁶he took the seven loaves and the fish; and after giving thanks he broke them and gave them to the disciples, and the disciples gave them to the crowds. ³⁷And all of them ate & were filled; and they took up the broken pieces left over, seven baskets full. ³⁸Those who had eaten were four thousand men, besides women & children. ³⁹After sending away the crowds, he got into the boat and went to the region of Magadan.

¹³ Now when Jesus came into the district of Caesarea Philippi, he asked his disciples, "Who do people say that the Son of Man is?" ¹⁴And they said, "Some say John the Baptist, but others Elijah, & still others Jeremiah or one of the prophets." ¹⁵He said to them,

PETER'S CONFESSION

How are these two stories related to each other through the illuminations?

These two illuminations are a good example of the way believers have interpreted many of the passages in Matthew's Gospel. From the early days of Christianity, the calming of the storm was seen as a metaphor for the salvation of those following Christ. Likewise, Jesus' promise at Peter's confession, that the gates of Hades will not prevail upon the community of the faithful, has provided hope to Christians in distress.

The five dramatic verses where Jesus calms the storm come in the middle of a longer passage. The main focus of chapters 8 and 9 are the miraculous healings Jesus is performing. In the illumination, the movement is from roiling sea to a serene and abstract construction. This pale blue background seems crowned in gold, with shapes that call to mind church arches and windows. After rebuking the apostles for their lack of faith, Jesus rebukes the storm. What is the message here for how the church should live in times of trouble? What is the message about the relationship between miracles and faith?

At Matthew 16, Jesus is portrayed in gold as the revealed Messiah in this triptych, or three-part image. At the right some see the face of Peter. There is a human face there, but the cubist style makes the face seem built of rock, reflecting the words of Jesus: "on this rock I will build my church" (16:18). The image includes crosses and fragments of flags. The flags reappear in the illumination at Acts 1, Pentecost, and connect the illuminations on the church to Saint John's University, where bright flags fly at special events. The connection between the revelation of the messiah and the crucifixion is made in the cross. In this same passage Jesus tells the apostles he must suffer and die, and Peter's reaction receives a strong rebuke. Jesus' head is also framed not just by a halo but a cross.

The left section of the illumination is based on a historical description of the place where Peter made his confession,

Calming of the Storm and Peter's Confession

MATTHEW 8:23-27 /
MATTHEW 16:13-23
What sort of man is this, that even the winds and the sea obey him? (8:27)

at the foot of Mount Heron in Caesarea Philippi, a religious center of the Greco-Roman world. One of the sources of the Jordan River issued from a large cave at the site. During Jesus' time the area was under the control of a son of Herod the Great, Herod Philip, who constructed there his palace and a temple to Pan, the Greek god of the forest and the underworld. The cave opening where the waters emerged was believed to be an opening to the underworld. It is here that Jesus says: "I will build my church, and the gates of Hades will not prevail against it" (16:18).

The vision of hell in this illumination combines several elements. It is identified by the Hebrew word for the underworld, "Sheol," has a representation of Assyrian gods (the eagle-beaked, winged horse), and a microscopic view of the AIDS virus, a contemporary vision of the experience of hell. What other figures do you see in each of the three parts of this illumination? What do they tell us about Jesus and the church?

Marginalia AT MATTHEW CHAPTERS 11–14

On the pages between these two major illuminations are some excellent examples of the marginal ornamentation in *The Saint John's Bible*. On the page for Matthew 11 is one of Chris Tomlin's insects, a dragonfly. On the next page, in the margin of Matthew 14, is a mandala and also some key marginal notes.

Marginalia, any writing on the border of a page, was common in medieval and renaissance manuscripts. Marginalia could be commentary or decoration. Often the copyist monks would personalize the manuscripts by drawing fanciful decorations in the margins. Later readers might make a note on the text, as many people do when using textbooks.

At the same time, the integrity of the Bible text was very important to everyone involved. In fact, at some periods of history even the artwork became regulated, with certain archetypes always used for certain passages. The decoration also reflected the cultural situation at the time. For exam-

THE ART OF THE SAINT JOHN'S BIBLE

ple, in 1131 the Cistercians, an order of monks that broke off from the Benedictine tradition, issued a decree that initials marking a transition from one chapter to another should be in one color, and should contain no human or animal figures (a decree that was widely ignored)!

Marginalia is just one more piece of the history of the manuscript, created by hand and passed from hand to hand as a source of wisdom and knowledge as well as a source of pleasure and spiritual reflection.

The marginalia in *The Saint John's Bible* is decorative and enhances the aesthetic pleasure of the volumes. The dragonfly is common to Collegeville and throughout Minnesota, like the butterflies in other margins. The mandala here is also called an arabesque. Arabesques derived from Islamic art were common to illuminated manuscripts. Its presence here is casual and decorative, a sign that the copyist took a pause, as we ask readers of the Bible to pause and reflect along the way.

The notes on the text correspond to the NRSV, the translation of the Bible chosen for *The Saint John's Bible*. These notes, referenced by small red letters in the body of the text, give alternative translations of specific words in the Greek text, point to differences between ancient manuscripts, define significant names given in Hebrew or Greek, and otherwise offer helpful information on the text.

Above these notes are a small cross and the letters "RSB" in red, along with the citation Matt 13:52. If you look at the verse, you'll see a corresponding cross in the margin below the verse number 51. These notes refer to Bible citations found in the Rule of Benedict, tying the book again to the Benedictines of Saint John's Abbey. There are 126 biblical citations in the Rule of Benedict, a very large number for such a brief document. Reading the Bible is central to Benedictine spirituality, including the practice of *lectio divina*. In this form of prayer, the reader dwells meditatively on a text, usually the Bible, reading it slowly several times and letting it reveal multiple meanings and significance. A process much like *lectio divina* was used by Donald Jackson and the

RSB
Matt 13:52

p Gk: hid in
q Other ancient authorities read *the prophet Isaiah*
r Other ancient authorities lack *of the world*
s Other ancient authorities add *to hear*
t Gk: *them*
u Gk: *tetrarch*
v Other ancient authorities read *his brother's wife*
w Gk: *he*

members of the Committee on Illumination and Text in determining and developing all the artwork for this Bible. Following these markers, you may begin to see a pattern for monastic life emerging from the text.

You will notice one other feature in the margins as you go through the gospel text. Turn back to Matthew 6–8, the Sermon on the Mount. In the margin you'll see a word that appears to be in Hebrew, followed by a small red diamond. The word is actually in Aramaic, a language that looks a lot like Hebrew. The red diamond can be found in Matthew 6:25. In the NRSV text, the verse quotes Jesus saying, "You cannot serve God and wealth." The NRSV note, signified by the small red letter 'a,' explains that the Greek text has the word "mammon" instead of "wealth." It is a familiar verse most of us know from the King James Version: "Ye cannot serve God and mammon." Mammon is actually an Aramaic word. The Committee on Illumination and Text decided that the Aramaic words that appear in the gospels would appear in the margins in their original.

Another good example is found at Matthew 27:45. Here the NRSV has kept the Aramaic, and when Jesus dies on the cross he cries out, "Eli, Eli, lema sabachthani?" which is then translated as "My God, my God, why have you forsaken me?" In the margin is the actual Aramaic text. Again, when Jesus opens the ears of the deaf man in Mark 7:32-35, he says, "Ephphatha," which means "be opened." The Aramaic text is in the margin. Most often, the NRSV has kept the Aramaic word in its translation, but even when a translation is given ("wealth" for "mammon," or "my teacher" for "Rabbouni" in Mark 10:51), *The Saint John's Bible* gives the Aramaic in the margin.

What do you make of this representation of the Last Judgment and Second Coming?

MATTHEW 24–25
Then the kingdom of God will be like this. (25:1)

In this extensive passage from the Gospel of Matthew, Jesus lays out a vision of the end of the age and of his return. The illumination has great similarities to the Confession of Peter, in terms of color and image and even composition. There is a great deal of darkness and chaos in the first part of the image, but that is not the focus of the miniature.

The central portion, with its sweeping arches and open spaces, its circular motion and gold of divine presence, is the heart of the image. The cross and the circle come together, an image of the reconciling action of the crucifixion. To the right are more circles bisected by crosses, and at the bottom rises a refreshing patch of green foliage. We live in the period between Jesus' resurrection and his return, as did the church of Matthew.

What lies beyond this moment? Again we see the use of images from earlier miniatures, the gold filaments stamped at the top, the white fragment of an arch. What do Christians do to further the reign of God? The boundaries between the dark times of chaos are sharp, but not so the movement from the central panel to the right.

Suzanne Moore created this illumination and the one at Matthew 8:23-26 depicting the calming of the storm. All the illuminations in Matthew, then, convey in one way or another what it means that the Messiah has broken into history. The Genealogy, Beatitudes, Calming of the Storm, Peter's Confession, and this image of the Last Judgment, all present a vision of Christ as the New Covenant, defeating death and chaos. This might explain the sharp distinction between the dark, swirling first panel and the gold arcs, compared to the more subtle shift to the final panel. Jesus' death and resurrection defeat death and chaos altogether. The coming of the kingdom, however, is more gradual.

There is still another way to read this image, if we see the left side of the illumination as a representation of the world. The right side of the image uses the same colors as

3 another; all will be thrown down." ∎ When he was sitting on the Mount of Olives, the disciples came to him privately, saying, "Tell us, when will this be, & what will be the sign of your coming and of the end of the age?" ⁴ Jesus answered them, "Beware that no one leads you astray.⁵ For many will come in my name, saying, 'I am the Messiah!' and they will lead many astray. ⁶ And you will hear of wars and rumors of wars; see that you are not alarmed; for this must take place; but the end is not yet.
⁷ For nation will rise against nation, and kingdom against kingdom, and there will be famines and earthquakes in various places;⁸ all this is but the
9 beginning of the birth pangs. ∎ "Then they will hand you over to be tortured and will put you to death, and you will be hated by all nations because of my name.¹⁰ Then many will fall away, and they will betray one another & hate one another. ¹¹ And many false prophets will arise & lead many astray.
¹²And because of the increase of lawlessness, the love of many will grow cold.¹³ But the one who endures to the end will be saved.¹⁴ And this good news of the kingdom will be proclaimed through-out the world, as a testimony to all the nations; and
15 then the end will come. ∎ "So when you see the desolating sacrilege standing in the holy place, as was spoken of by the prophet Daniel (let the reader understand),¹⁶ then those in Judea must flee to the mountains;¹⁷ the one on the housetop must not go down to take what is in the house;¹⁸ the one in the field must not turn back to get a coat. ¹⁹ (Woe to

those who are pregnant & to those who are nursing infants in those days! ²⁰ Pray that your flight may not be in winter or on a sabbath.²¹ For at that time there will be great suffering, such as has not been from the beginning of the world until now, no, and never will be.²²And if those days had not been cut short, no one would be saved; but for the sake of the elect those days will be cut short. ²³ Then if any one says to you, 'Look! Here is the Messiah!' or 'There he is!'—do not believe it.²⁴ For false messiahs and false prophets will appear and produce great signs and omens, to lead astray, if possible, even the elect. ²⁵ Take note, I have told you beforehand.²⁶ So, if they say to you, 'Look! He is in the wilderness,' do not go out. If they say, 'Look! He is in the inner rooms,' do not believe it.²⁷ For as the lightning comes from the east & flashes as far as the west, so will be the coming of the Son of Man.²⁸ Wherever the corpse
29 is, there the vultures will gather. ∎ "Immediately after the suffering of those days

the sun will be darkened,
and the moon will not give its light;
the stars will fall from heaven,
and the powers of heaven will be shaken.

³⁰ Then the sign of the Son of Man will appear in heaven, & then all the tribes of the earth will mourn, & they will see 'the Son of Man coming on the clouds of heaven' with power and great glory. ³¹ And he will send out his angels with a loud trumpet call, and they will gather his elect from the four winds,
32 from one end of heaven to the other. ∎ "From the

the left, although the quality and effect is very different. This continuity suggests not a break from the world as it is, but a transformation.

None of us can possibly know what the Last Judgment will be like. Jesus' words here are not a literal prediction of future events, but use a variety of literary styles: parable for the story of the bridesmaids, apocalyptic poetry for its account of signs in the sky, prophetic formulas that echo Isaiah and Jeremiah. In the same way, the illumination suggests and represents the theological truth: the old order of sin and chaos shall come to an end, and the kingdom of God shall be present in its place.

❡ Does this image reflect your sense of the passage in Matthew? What other pieces of the text do you see here?

Baptism of Jesus

MARK 1:9-11 *And just as he was coming up out of the water, he saw the heavens torn apart and the Spirit descending like a dove on him. (1:10)*

Where do you see the markers of humanity and divinity, the two worlds of heaven and earth, and how do they come together in this illumination?

John the Baptist is the patron of Saint John's Abbey, and so it was important to give him a strong presence in the illuminations. Mark's Gospel is the one account which states that John actually baptizes Jesus. Although Luke's Gospel covers the ministry of John the Baptist more extensively, it is here that Jesus is revealed as God's beloved son. This passage gave Donald Jackson the basis for a complex and exuberant illumination.

At the front of the frame is the Baptist. The fact that it is John the Baptist and not Jesus who is the focus of this illumination is itself unusual. Notice his hands and feet. He moves forward, and he gestures in invitation, even as he looks back. He is not contained by the frame of the image. He is the Forerunner, placed before the image depicting the main event. His gaze backwards is not to the past, but to the scene of the baptism itself, the story he was sent to proclaim. In the scene are many figures: a crowd on shore, others in the water, and Jesus truly rising up, almost indistinguishable from the gold swatches surrounding him.

The sky is indeed open, and angels much like those in the illumination of Jacob's ladder, descend and ascend. More angels—or are they birds?—circle the heavens in blue. Remember the special properties of birds we discussed in Genesis 1, metaphorically linking the divine and human worlds.

The image is not without darkness. Red eyes peer out from the left-hand side, along with two large spiders. These images introduce the temptation awaiting Jesus in the desert. According to the text, after the baptism Jesus heads immediately into the desert, where he is tempted for forty days and nights. John the Baptist is not a celebratory figure in this scene, but somber, as though he sees more deeply into the revelation of Jesus' divinity. Above John is also the stamped figure of the church, a reflection of the larger ministry and the role of baptism as initiation in the church.

❧ What else does this scene suggest?

THE ART OF THE SAINT JOHN'S BIBLE

BAPTISM OF JESUS

Parable of the Sower and the Seed

MARK 4:3-9 *He began to teach them many things in parables, and in his teaching he said to them: "Listen! A sower went out to sow." (4:3)*

Who is the Sower in this miniature? Does the image match the parable?

The parable of the sower is one of the images in the New Testament painted with techniques associated with the Eastern Church and its iconography. This was done in part to honor the common heritage that the churches of the East and West share, but also to acknowledge the precious visual language that the Eastern Church has developed to express theological concepts and doctrine. Also interesting is that a maker of icons is said to "write" an icon, not to paint it. We don't usually think of someone writing a picture. In what way does this tradition demand that we see differently?

This approach has resulted in one of the most popular illuminations, but it also introduced many issues that were avoided in some of the more "free" approaches to other texts. Who, asked the Committee on Illumination and Text, should be the figure of the sower? He is understood to be a metaphor for Christ's ministry sowing the Word. But Christ himself is the Word being sown. How then should the sower be shown? Parables, walking the line between allegory, metaphor, and narrative, don't break open neatly.

This image solves the problem by allowing the paradox to be experienced by combining different traditions into one image. The basic style of the image is that of the sacred icon and the face of the sower is that of Christ. We are looking, therefore, at a sacred, symbolic action, not just a farming scene. On the other hand, the artist has clothed this Christ in ordinary Western work clothes, jeans and a sweatshirt. We are also called to sow the seed, just as we are called to be receptive ground for the seed to grow in us. Icons are meant to open up our understanding of the sacred, just as they paradoxically tie them to a concrete image. Is this image showing us Christ or God the Father (who cannot be imaged)? Yes and no. Are the seeds the works of Christ or Christ himself being given for the salvation of the world? The answer is not one or the other, but "both and." (Notice how the seed scatters across the page into the text itself.)

THE ART OF THE SAINT JOHN'S BIBLE

◖ How can we read the image, or for that matter, the parable? To paraphrase the gospel: Let those who have eyes, look!

4

PARABLE OF THE SOWER AND THE SEED

Two Cures

MARK 5:25-43

She had heard about Jesus, and came up behind him in the crowd and touched his cloak, for she said, "If I but touch his clothes, I will be made well." (5:27-28)

TWO CURES

Why do you think the artist showed the healing miracles this way, rather than with a dramatic image of someone before and after being healed?

Iconography is employed again in the story of the healing of the woman with hemorrhages and the daughter of the leader at the synagogue. The panels make great use of the structure of the story. The woman who touches the hem of his garment appears as he is going to the girl's home. A story of faith is inserted inside a story of faith. A woman who is unclean is bold in reaching out to touch Jesus. Jairus travels from the synagogue to where Jesus is to get him to lay hands on his daughter so that she may be healed. Observe Jesus' hands in the illustrations. In the first he makes a sign of blessing, in the second he holds up his cloak, from which power has gone out, and in the third he grasps the wrist of the girl, while again making the sign of blessing.

In these images, also, Jesus is surrounded. The boy in the crowd breaks the frame of the second panel, showing how large the crowd is that surrounds him. Three figures join him in the other panels, old and young, of different levels of status.

In what way does this image illustrate two stories?
In what way does it unify them?

Mark's Gospel has not one but two accounts of the multiplication of loaves and fishes. In the first, Jesus feeds five thousand and in the second, four thousand. These are often interpreted as being about the salvation message extended to both the Jews and the Gentiles, and the subtly different coloring between the left panel and right illustrate the movement from the twelve tribes of Israel to the Gentiles, both recipients of the bountiful gifts of God.

Originally this was planned as a quarter page illumination, but clearly the artwork as well as the food was multiplied! The imagery is so rich, and so central in Christianity: the desert places, the fishermen apostles, the breaking and blessing of bread, the gathering up of the remnants. The fish and bread have a prominent place in the illustration, the bread rendered in gold and marked by the cross to link it to the eucharistic bread. Do you also see the little brown bars and angles like pieces of bread scattered around the page, or the scale-like marks representing the pieces of fish? The fish and bread images are inspired by a Byzantine mosaic from Tabgha, a spot on the shore of the Sea of Galilee where tradition locates this miracle.

The basket designs swirling around the illumination have their origin in ancient Native American Anasazi basketry. Like the mandala images throughout *The Saint John's Bible*, the spiral on the basket appealed to Donald Jackson and here suggested the exponential multiplication of the miracle. The image connects the Bible again to the American setting, but more important to Jackson, the baskets connect to the dizzying sense of the miracle, and are "sacred geometry."

The multiple layers of imagery here refer to the overwhelming gifts of a prodigal God. Donald Jackson described the way these gifts radiate into the human community this way: "My understanding is that every act of sharing or goodwill multiplies itself. I want to try to establish a

Loaves and Fishes

MARK 6:33-44; 8:1-10
"Taking the five loaves and the two fish, he looked up to heaven, and blessed and broke the loaves, and gave them to his disciples to set before the people; and he divided the two fish among them all. And all ate and were filled." (Mark 6:41-42)

others said, "It is a prophet, like one of the prophets of old." But when Herod heard of it, he said, "John, whom I beheaded, has been raised." For Herod himself had sent men who arrested John, bound him, and put him in prison on account of Herodias, his brother Philip's wife, because Herod had married her. For John had been telling Herod, "It is not lawful for you to have your brother's wife." And Herodias had a grudge against him, and wanted to kill him. But she could not, for Herod feared John, knowing that he was a righteous and holy man, and he protected him. When he heard him, he was greatly perplexed; and yet he liked to listen to him. But an opportunity came when Herod on his birthday gave a banquet for his courtiers and officers & for the leaders of Galilee. When his daughter Herodias came in & danced, she pleased Herod & his guests; and the king said to the girl, "Ask me for whatever you wish, and I will give it." And he solemnly swore to her, "Whatever you ask me, I will give you, even half of my kingdom." She went out and said to her mother, "What should I ask for?" She replied, "The head of John the baptizer." Immediately she rushed back to the king and requested, "I want you to give me at once the head of John the Baptist on a platter." The king was deeply grieved; yet out of regard for his oaths and for the guests, he did not want to refuse her. Immediately the king sent a soldier of the guard with orders to bring John's head. He went and beheaded him in the prison, brought his head on a platter, and gave it to the girl. Then the girl gave it to her mother. When his disciples heard about it, they came and took his body, and laid it in a tomb.

The apostles gathered around Jesus, and told him all that they had done and taught. He said to them, "Come away to a deserted place all by yourselves and rest a while." For many were coming and going, and they had no leisure even to eat. And they went away in the boat to a deserted place by themselves. Now many saw them going and recognized them, and they hurried there on foot from all the towns and arrived ahead of them. As he went ashore, he saw a great crowd; and he had compassion for them, because they were like sheep without a shepherd; and he began to teach them many

He left that place and came to his home town, and his disciples followed him. On the sabbath he began to teach in the synagogue, & many who heard him were astounded. They said, "Where did this man get all this? What is this wisdom that has been given to him? What deeds of power are being done by his hands! Is not this the carpenter, the son of Mary & brother of James and Joses & Judas & Simon, and are not his sisters here with us?" And they took offense at him. Then Jesus said to them, "Prophets are not without honor, except in their hometown, and among their own kin, and in their own house." And he could do no deed of power there, except that he laid his hands on a few sick people and cured them. And he was amazed at their unbelief.

Then he went about among the villages teaching. He called the twelve and began to send them out two by two, and gave them authority over the unclean spirits. He ordered them to take nothing for their journey except a staff; no bread, no bag, no money in their belts; but to wear sandals and not to put on two tunics. He said to them, "Wherever you enter a house, stay there until you leave the place. If any place will not welcome you and they refuse to hear you, as you leave, shake off the dust that is on your feet as a testimony against them." So they went out and proclaimed that all should repent. They cast out many demons, & anointed with oil many who were sick and cured them. King Herod heard of it; for Jesus' name had become known. Some were saying, "John the baptizer has been raised from the dead; and for this reason these powers are at work in him." But others said, "It is Elijah."

sense of multiplicity of the exponential acts of love, sharing, or charity." In that way the image flows around the page like the flow of love. The blue batons, meant to give the design fixed points, also serve as obstacles to this movement. In Jackson's words, "they represent sins of commis-

THE ART OF THE SAINT JOHN'S BIBLE

sion, moments when our actions interrupt the flow of love." Sins of omission are represented by blank spots, "times we should act with love but don't."

❦ How do the human and divine come together in this story and illumination?

THE TRANSFIGURATION

THE ART OF THE SAINT JOHN'S BIBLE

How does this illumination compare to the way you imagine the Transfiguration?

For a second time God's voice comes from heaven to announce, "This is my Son, the Beloved" (v. 7). Look at the faces of Moses and Elijah, wonderfully rendered by iconographer Aidan Hart in this collaboration with Donald Jackson. How is the expression of Moses different from his expression at the end of Deuteronomy in *Pentateuch*, where he was looking into the Promised Land? How else can we recognize him—in the colors and brush strokes of his robe? In that earlier illumination Moses took center stage, but here his role pointing to the Christ is clear.

Moses holds two tablets, as religious figures in medieval and renaissance paintings often hold a symbol of their identity. Compare this illumination also to its counterpoint at the beginning of Mark's Gospel, the first place God announced his Son. There are similarities in the brush strokes and other elements. There is no border to this image. The crosses in the background of the John frontispiece, The Word Made Flesh, are the same as in Christ's robe here. The blue of the sky and the purple of the earth give more gravity to the concrete world where the event takes place. The sky in the Transfiguration looks like the sea in earlier illuminations in Matthew and Mark, or like the sky in the baptism. Peter is wrong to think Elijah and Moses are equal to Jesus, but he is right that this is sacred ground.

Unlike the frightened apostles, we have insight into the Christ who is here revealed. The painting goes even further than our ordinary imagination might. We are likely to imagine three figures, more or less the same, but with Jesus in a white robe instead of blue or red. This illumination says no, Jesus is transfigured, his glory is revealed. If you look closely at his robe, you will see it is not an ordinary garment like the one worn by Moses and Elijah—it appears kingly, perhaps more like priestly vestments. His clothed body is fully there, but it is dazzling, gold shot through with white crosses, a representation of all that is being revealed. What draws

The Transfiguration

MARK 9:2-8
And his clothes became dazzling white, such as no one on earth could bleach them. And there appeared to them Elijah with Moses, who were talking with Jesus. (9:3-4)

our attention most, however, is his face. Both present and absent, dazzling but piercing us with his gaze, what do you make of this vision of God's Son?

When they descend the mountain, we are told in verse 15 that "when the whole crowd saw [Jesus], they were immediately overcome with awe, and they ran forward to greet him." Do they also get a glimpse of what has been revealed on the mountain? "Listen to Him" is repeated three times, first faintly on the bottom of the illumination, then across the page, and finally in a special text treatment by Sally Mae Joseph before the parables of Mark 12. Everything is pointing to the revelation of Christ in the world.

❡ Returning to the passage, how do we respond to Jesus when he is revealed to us in the midst of our ordinary lives?

How is this illumination of butterflies in their various states helpful in understanding the two endings of Mark's Gospel?

If you begin at the first verse of Mark 16 and read, you see how jarring it is to end at the first part of verse 8: "So they went out and fled from the tomb, for terror and amazement had seized them; and they said nothing to anyone, for they were afraid." Ending on a note of fear, before Jesus has been seen by the disciples, before the disciples have been commissioned and sent out, before Jesus' ascension into heaven, is dissatisfying. It was dissatisfying to the early community who used this gospel, and they were the ones presumably who added to the ending the two passages we see here. A third version is given in red in the margin under the footnote for verse 8b. It seems no one could leave this gospel alone. Whether the ending of the original manuscript of Mark was lost or the manuscript actually ended this abruptly is unknown, but the endings presented here were composed very early and have long been part of the accepted Bible.

Monarch butterflies, here rendered by Chris Tomlin, are often symbols of resurrection. The three stages of their life—caterpillar, chrysalis, and butterfly—correspond to life, death, and resurrection. Monarchs are prevalent in the Minnesota landscape surrounding Saint John's Abbey.

❦ Do you make any other connections between this image and the page?

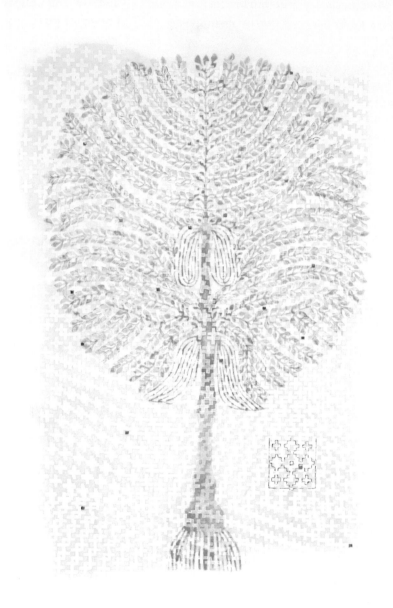

LUKE CARPET PAGE

THE ART OF THE SAINT JOHN'S BIBLE

The nearly blank page that follows the ending of the Gospel of Mark is called a carpet page, due to the similarity between the decoration on these pages and Oriental carpets. It is not left blank, but is also not particularly decorative. It may seem like a waste of a page, but carpet pages serve an important purpose. The carpet page allows for a distinct space between one gospel and the next. In *The Saint John's Bible*, the carpet pages are lightly stamped and stenciled by Sally Mae Joseph from patterns she designed. Joseph has been one of the main calligraphers for the text of the Bible and has worked regularly at the Hendre, the studio (called a scriptorium) for the production of the Bible in Wales.

The pattern here can also be called a "diaper pattern," from the French word *diapré* meaning variegated. In the Middle Ages the term applied to woven fabrics, and later to repetitive geometric patterns stamped on fabrics. Many of Joseph's patterns are derived from textiles. They can be found not just on the carpet pages but throughout the volumes.

Carpet pages are neutral, to provide the eye with a visual pause before embarking on the next gospel and heavy illumination. Like traditional carpet pages, these are textured and add richness to the treatment of the gospels without being distracting. This page is vertical, mirroring the monarch illumination on the previous page. The carpet page at the end of the Gospel of Luke, "The Tree of Life," is more figurative, and also reminiscent of the interlocking forms and circles found in the Book of Kells and Lindisfarne Gospels, two other famous illuminated manuscripts. The Tree of Life design was translated from an appliqued bedspread from India.

Carpet pages also serve an important purpose by veiling full page illuminations. Vellum pages are somewhat translucent, and without the design of the carpet page you might be left with unsightly "show-through" from the heavy illumination at the beginning of the Book of Luke.

The Birth of Christ

LUKE 2:1-20

And she gave birth to her firstborn son and wrapped him in bands of cloth, and laid him in a manger, because there was no place for them in the inn. (2:7)

What unusual images do you see in this nativity scene? Why do you think they are here?

This frontispiece for Luke draws us into the seasons of Advent and Christmas, where Luke's account of the nativity is the focus. The revelation of the divine is seen in the shaft of gold coming from the manger, into which peer Mary, shepherds, and one of the kings. Notice their expressions of awe and wonder, and Mary's intimate leaning in and wise smile. The shepherds are women and children, one holding a small child. This was probably the reality in the time of Jesus' birth. Remember also that David was a young shepherd, and Rachel met Jacob when she was watering her father's sheep at the well. Shepherds and sheep, like the ram in front, play an important role not just in this story but throughout the Old and New Testaments.

Again the illumination has many sections that you can "read," finding echoes to other illuminations: the angels from Jacob's ladder, the filigree from the Transfiguration, the stars from Abraham's covenant. All that has been promised is being fulfilled; God is revealed to humanity; the two worlds are bridged. At the forefront of the scene are the animals. All the figures circling the manger draw our attention to the coexistence of the earthly and the spiritual in this event. The donkey and the ram are easy to relate to a biblical context. In addition to the parables of the sheep and the metaphor of Jesus as the Good Shepherd, there is the ram given in the place of Isaac as a sacrifice back in Genesis. Jesus will also be our sacrificial lamb. Jesus will enter Jerusalem on a donkey on Palm Sunday, another connection between the birth and Passion. The vertical shaft of light from the manger, together with the horizontal line of angels, makes the figure of the cross. This image also reminds us that the crucifixion is tied to the birth, the reason Christ came. Additionally, it connects to the ancient legend that the wood of Christ's crib was used to make his cross.

But what do you make of the ox? This ox is modeled on one of the Neolithic cave paintings of great aurochs at Lascaux, France. Does it make you think of the song "Away in the Manger" and the line: "The cattle are lowing"? In traditional Christian art, each of the evangelists is assigned a figure. Medieval manuscripts are often stamped or illustrated with these figures. Matthew is represented by a man, Mark a lion, John an eagle, and Luke an ox, which we see here at the beginning of his gospel. Some have pointed out that the manger looks like a book cover. It is actually rendered in the "reverse perspective" style of icon paintings. In "linear perspective" drawing, which we are used to, the front of the manger would be wider than the back, because the back is farther away from us. In Byzantine icons, however, the opposite is true. Compare this to the illumination of the Christian community at Acts 4. The altar there has the same shape and perspective as this manger. All these associations are helpful, and draw attention to the purpose of all four gospels, which is to make the glory of God known. God as altar, God as Word, and God as infant in a manger are just some of the images that come together for those who meditate on the illumination.

◀ What do you see?

THE BIRTH OF CHRIST

Chrysography

LUKE 1:46-55

Unlike Matthew, Mark, and John, the book of Luke has no decorated incipit, or beginning. The first paragraph is set off from the rest of the text, but it is not in a different script. The initial is no more elaborate than those beginning other chapters, and in some ways less elaborate. Our attention is on the illumination of the Nativity, whose text is in chapter 2. When we turn the page, however, we encounter three major text treatments.

The Magnificat, which is Mary's reply to Elizabeth, is one of the great hymns of the church. It is sung daily at evening prayer by the Benedictines of Saint John's Abbey. The tradition of chrysography, the Greek term for "writing in gold," goes back to Early Christianity. In these treatments the text was written in gesso with a quill before being gilded with gold leaf and burnished. In ancient times purple was also significant. Pages of dyed purple parchment are found in Byzantine books as early as the sixth century. It was a color that signified royalty and wealth. Plus, it showed off the gold! There was no higher text treatment than gold writing on purple background.

The Canticle of Zechariah is also an important Christian hymn, and it is recited as part of the Liturgy of Hours at morning prayer. The third canticle, that of Simeon, appears in blue at Luke 2:29-32 and is recited at compline, the last set of prayers for the day. These special treatments are another connection between the liturgy of the church and the text of the Bible.

THE ART OF THE SAINT JOHN'S BIBLE

What distinguishes the left side of this illumination from the right? What unites them?

The illuminations for the Gospel of Luke focus on story. It is in this gospel we get a long story of Jesus' nativity, along with the story of John the Baptist's birth, visits and visitations, and canticles. Also in Luke are a collection of beloved parables. The quarter-page illumination of the dinner at the Pharisee's house was designated by the Committee on Illumination and Text because of the themes of forgiveness and salvation, and the charge made against Jesus that he too often associated with sinners.

We have no reason to think poorly of Simon in this story. Even Jesus says that he is a good person, like the one who has a small debt to be forgiven. The woman, however, is a

Dinner at the Pharisee's House

LUKE 7:36-50
She stood behind him at his feet, weeping, and began to bathe his feet with her tears and to dry them with her hair. Then she continued kissing his feet and anointing them with the ointment. (7:38)

DINNER AT THE PHARISEE'S HOUSE

gate-crasher, an interloper, and a known sinner. She brings chaos into the household, which Donald Jackson represents here by the messy and upset elements of the tidy household. The words of Christ in the middle of the scene mediate between the chaos the woman has created and her intense focus on her task, which is to express her love. Does the viewer see the love or chaos? Do we prefer the tidy household or the intensity of love?

The strong black line dividing the illumination represents the chasm between the world of the sinful woman and that of the Pharisees. On the line rests a whole circle, like a halo or church window, another mandala, apparent on both sides of the illumination. What is holiness? How is it related to love? The woman is represented as unconventional, wildly dressed, her hair in green and pink. The world that the woman has put in disarray is symbolized by the scarf, on which Hebrew words are written related to rituals of temple sacrifice. The scarf stretched across the image makes another kind of border; the conventional world, in every place and time, is never receptive to those on the margins. Here, that world attempts to block this marginal woman from access to Jesus. However, the scarf is crumpled, disrupted by the uninvited guest. "You gave me no kiss," Christ says to the Pharisee (v. 45). The reproach highlights the woman's action—"she has shown great love" (v. 47). She has recognized what it means that her sins are forgiven, and responded out of that realization.

Think about the similarities and differences between this illumination and those in Matthew and Mark. In Matthew, Christ calms the seas and conquers death and chaos. In this story it is love that is chaotic, disrupting a world whose order is empty. The illumination of the Loaves and Fishes in Mark also shows the same kind of messy overflowing and abundance of Christ's love. When God breaks into history as Jesus Christ, there is a disruption of the world in its usual state. The next major illumination, the Parables, builds on this theme, with more examples of God's abundant love and forgiveness.

THE ART OF THE SAINT JOHN'S BIBLE

Do you have a favorite parable illuminated here? What does the illumination add to the story?

Jesus taught with parables, and this anthology page captures some of the most beloved parables in the Gospel of Luke. At the right are Martha and Mary listening to Jesus, and the words, "There is need of only one thing," from Luke 10:42. That one thing is to listen, and Mary has chosen the better part. Here Martha stands in her apron with hands on hips and looks impatient, but at the same time she is, like her sister seated beside her, also gazing at the Lord. Martha and Mary are two sides of love and care, two images of hospitality, a value that is central to the Benedictine tradition. The Rule of Benedict instructs the monks to welcome all visitors as Christ. The parables portrayed here are all about love and care as well.

The Parable of the Good Samaritan is represented by text from the story. We hear of those who passed by, and of the Samaritan who stopped. These quotations draw attention to the sectarian nature of the tale—the priest and Levite both have high status within Judaism. Priests would be at the top of the social hierarchy, and served at the temple, but Levites were descendants of the tribe of Israel, set aside as priests and charged with special duties. The Samaritan, on the other hand, is lower even than tax collectors and sinners, seen as ethnically inferior, thought to have no privileged relationship to God or understanding of what is good. At the center is a vision of compassion: "[A Samaritan] was moved . . . and bandaged his wounds" (vv. 33-34). This quote leads our eye to the image in gold of the Twin Towers. Why do you think this image is in gold? Why is it located here between the Parables of the Lost Son, the Good Samaritan, and Dives and Lazarus?

"The parable [of the Lost Son] is all about forgiveness," said Donald Jackson. He used the image of the Twin Towers as a contemporary example of the challenge of forgiving evil. "You're really challenged to overcome your anger. It's got to be really difficult to forgive." It is an example, he

Luke Anthology

LUKE 10:38-42
Jesus with Mary and Martha

LUKE 10:29-37
The Good Samaritan

LUKE 15:4-7
The Lost Sheep

LUKE 15:8-10
The Lost Coin

LUKE 15:11-32
The Lost Son

LUKE 16:19-31
Lazarus and Dives

So he told them this parable . . . (15:3)

LUKE ANTHOLOGY

said, "representing the difficulty of achieving pure, unreasonable love." In the parable, we see a father's love for his wayward son, here painted by Aidan Hart, but what a radical step to apply that same love to the entire human family? The Good Samaritan is this kind of story, too: love that passes boundaries, love for the other, without fear.

How else is the theme of lost and found played out in this illumination? Nine ghostly coins dance around the moonlike lost coin. Which is more precious? The lost sheep

looks from darkness toward the angels and God's love. What do you think of this sheep? It is not moving toward the light, but needs the shepherd to come even farther to re-store its place with the others. Again we see divine love that goes beyond reason. Still, the illumination is not without a scene of judgment. At the bottom is Dives, the wealthy man who did not attend to the beggar Lazarus at his door. Now he claws at the banner scene—do you see a vision of those still on earth or of hell? He seems crushed by the weight of it, as he now asks Lazarus, finally comforted in the arms of Abraham, for assistance. Or has he wrenched the banner from its diagonal place as a sign of his desperation that the others be warned? Lazarus, meanwhile, is comforted by Abraham and tended to by angels. Above them is the Hebrew word 'Abraham,' taking us back to the genealogy of Matthew, reminding us of Christ's presence in all these stories.

Pieces of the mandala from Matthew's genealogy are here again, worked into the diagonals and border by Sally Mae Joseph. They are meant, according to Donald Jackson, to suggest the way the mind and intelligence work to interpret and understand concepts, like teasing out the meaning of parables and applying them to our contemporary lives.

❡ Now that you've explored the illumination, what are other aspects of the relationship between Martha and Mary and the parables?

How do you understand the three parts of this illumination?

Eucharist

LUKE 22:14-20
"This is my body, which is given for you. Do this in remembrance of me."
(22:19b)

The Last Supper has often been illustrated with the disciples gathered around Jesus at the table, as in Leonardo DaVinci's famous painting. This miniature focuses on the liturgical connection between the Passover meal celebrated by Jesus and the apostles and Christian eucharistic celebrations. It recognizes the connection between Passover and Eucharist, and also reflects Catholic and other Christian liturgies where this Bible passage forms the basis for prayers of consecration. The first panel shows the gifts brought forward, the unconsecrated bread and wine. They are brought as a sacrificial offering, and the people recite, "May the Lord accept this sacrifice."

In the center panel is the lamb that is at the heart of the Passover meal and story, also an image for Jesus as the sacrificial lamb. At the elevation, many Christian liturgies share the response, "This is the Lamb of God, who takes away the sins of the world." The cup with the wine is connected to the lamb by blood. The image draws us into a deeper sense of the body and blood nature of the mystery. As Jesus said at the Last Supper, "This is my body . . . This is my blood."

Finally there is the image of a ciborium, where the consecrated Eucharist is reserved for the sick and dying. The three images together present a theology of the celebration of Eucharist. As the passage reads, "This is my body, which is given for you. Do this in remembrance of me" (v. 19b). When Christians come together for Eucharist, it is a meal and a sacrifice, affirming faith and the new covenant.

THE CRUCIFIXION

Why do you think the creators of The Saint John's Bible *chose to illuminate the crucifixion in Luke's Gospel? Why did they use so much gold in this illumination?*

Looking backward and forward to the endings of the four gospels, you will see the emphasis on different aspects of Jesus' death and resurrection. In Matthew's Gospel Suzanne Moore's abstract illumination of the Last Judgment is the final major illumination. In Mark, where the text is fragmentary and disputed, we see the Monarch butterflies of resurrection. Looking forward to John, the meeting between the risen Jesus and Mary Magdalene is the focus. In the first century, many texts about Jesus were written. Only four made it to the official canon of the New Testament for widespread acceptance and use. It seems that to be included in the canon, the book had to tell the story of Christ's death and resurrection.

Luke's Gospel has both the story of the crucifixion and detailed accounts of Jesus' appearance to the disciples. The crucifixion is not the last major illumination, but is followed by a depiction of the disciples on the road to Emmaus. What is more, this illumination comes after we have encountered the revealed Christ in several significant ways: in the genealogy of Matthew, in Peter's Confession, the Last Judgment, his Baptism, Transfiguration, and the Birth of Christ. Each place that Jesus reveals his divinity, gold leaf was used. In the anthology of Luke, also, where God's radical love is taught, Jesus appears in the upper left hand in dazzling gold leaf. It is the idea of God showing himself in his divine love for humanity that the Gospel of Luke emphasizes.

Donald Jackson and the Committee on Illumination and Text have taken great care in the way they have represented Christ. The images vary, from the icon in workman's clothes for the Parable of the Sower, to the shaft of gold light emanating from the manger in Luke's nativity scene. This illumination also draws on traditional Christian representations and at the same time departs from that vision. In early sketches for the piece, Donald Jackson used the famous

The Crucifixion

LUKE 23:26-49
It was now about noon, and darkness came over the whole land until three in the afternoon, while the sun's light failed; and the curtain of the temple was torn in two. Then Jesus, crying with a loud voice, said, "Father, into your hands I commend my spirit." Having said this, he breathed his last. (12:44-46)

Gero Cross for the image of Christ. That cross, found in the cathedral in Cologne, Germany, is surrounded by an almond-shaped panel of gold (called in iconography a "mandorla") with rays radiating from it like a sunflower. The crucifixion with all its pain does not diminish the glory of God.

Other elements of the story are also represented. The left side shows the three hours of darkness and many moons, a reflection of the way the crucifixion brought about an end to time. Night and death are destroyed by this act, in the moment and for all time. The shreds of purple may represent the rending of the temple veil, the end not just of darkness but of earthly separation from God. Purple was luxurious, worn only by royalty or the wealthy. Here it also shows the destruction of worldly kingship and the establishment of Christ's kingdom. Another cross rises into the gold background, a reflection of the thief on the cross beside him. The procession on the lower right may be the procession of those saved by Christ's death and resurrection, or a reflection of the procession with the cross to Golgotha. The entire image breaks through the frame, a sign of how the crucifixion broke through the limits of the human world and of time.

LUKE 23:46

THE ART OF THE SAINT JOHN'S BIBLE

What elements of the story are emphasized in the illumination?

In some ways, this is the first story of the new community that would come to be known as Christians. Its elements are very much like the many stories in the Book of Acts which has been attributed to the same author. We find two disciples going out, sharing the story of Jesus with someone they meet on the road, receiving instruction while sitting under a tree, and then sharing a meal. These actions are all liturgical.

When the stranger breaks bread they recognize it is Jesus himself. In the illumination we see the two disciples, in much the same attitude as Mary and Martha, listening and gazing up at Jesus. There is a tree, reminiscent of the tree of life, one that we will see again in the images from Jesus' passion in the Resurrection illumination in John. It is representative of the Garden of Olives and the fact that here the disciples recount the story of Jesus' Passion to him on the road. There are also two images of Jesus, first as an unrecognizable stranger, and then breaking bread with the shadow of the cross behind him. Again we see the filament of gold patterned here and there, the presence of the church.

◀ How does the progression of the image, from top to bottom, tell us the meaning of the story?

Road to Emmaus

LUKE 24:13-36
While they were talking and discussing, Jesus himself came near and went with them, but their eyes were kept from recognizing him.
(24:15-16)

JESUS HIMSELF CAME NEAR
AND WENT WITH THEM
HE TOOK BREAD, BLESSED &
BROKE IT, & GAVE IT TO THEM:
THEN THEIR EYES WERE OPENED,
AND THEY RECOGNIZED HIM;
AND HE VANISHED
FROM THEIR SIGHT.

The Word Made Flesh

JOHN 1:1-14
In the beginning was the Word, and the Word was with God, and the Word was God. (1:1)

Which verses of these fourteen can you tie directly to the illumination?

The Committee on Illumination and Text saw in the prologue to the Gospel of John the biggest challenge of the four frontispiece illuminations. John's writings are more abstract than the other gospels, and contain some of the core ideas of Christian theology. Jesus is here "the Word" that was God and with God at the time of creation. He is also in this passage the Light of the World. John the Baptist is mentioned as the one who testified to him, but the focus is clearly on Jesus who had the power to bring people into the truth, in other words to reveal the nature of things through his words and his life.

The image here incorporates some of these key ideas. You will recognize the stencilled crosses from the Transfiguration illumination. The filigree we've seen before has also demonstrated the presence of the divine. How does this particular passage relate to Genesis and creation? The image of Christ seems to be stepping from the darkness which recalls the chaos and nothingness of the creation story and moves toward light and order. In fact, the texture behind Christ's head is inspired by an image taken from the Hubble Space Telescope and reflects the cosmic character of the event. To the left, a keyhole recalls the tradition of locked and hinged manuscripts securing, protecting, and holding the "key" to the Word of God. It might also make you think of standing at the door and knocking, of locked diaries, and of secret prayers of the heart.

The text in cursive script over the left side of the illumination is from Colossians 1:15-20. It expands on the announcement in John, that "The Word became flesh and lived among us" (v. 14). It connects the theology of reconciliation through the crucifixion and resurrection to the original creation and the final judgment, the alpha and omega:

> He is the image of the invisible God, the firstborn of all creation; for in him all things in heaven and on earth were created, things visible and invisible, whether thrones or domin-

ions or rulers or powers—all things have been created through him and for him. He himself is before all things, and in him all things hold together. He is the head of the body, the church; he is the beginning, the firstborn from the dead, so that he might come to have first place in everything. For in him all the fullness of God was pleased to dwell, and through him God was pleased to reconcile to himself all things, whether on earth or in heaven, by making peace through the blood of his cross.

◖ How do you conceptualize the idea that "the Word became flesh"?

THE WORD MADE FLESH

The Call of the Disciples

JOHN 1:35-51
He found Philip and said to him, "Follow me." (1:43)

What do you think is going on in the bottom right corner of this illumination?

What is your sense of the mood of this illumination? Why?

This illumination captures the crowds, the sense of purpose, and the joy of following Jesus. It is hard to pick out the figure of Christ, although he is at the center. He is painted in white, which connects him to the circling angels, but he also almost blends in with the people surrounding him. He is the same color as the angels, but he is also the same color as the lamb in the bottom right corner. The words of John the Baptist declare that Jesus is the Lamb of God. He is only called by this title twice in the gospels, both times in John, but it is important to our conception of Eucharist and Jesus as the Passover sacrifice. So it is that Eucharist images appear in this same corner of the illumination, along with a piece of cloth that can remind us of the liturgical nature of the event, or of any one of a number of associations we're building around these images. What do you make of the fact that the cloth breaks the boundary of the image? How are other important colors used in this miniature?

The Committee on Illumination and Text drew attention to the nature of the call in John's theology. "Discipleship has long been an important part of the Christian life, a concept which gained greater prominence with the life and writings of the twentieth century martyr, Dietrich Bonhoeffer." In this passage, "Two disciples hear [Jesus called the Lamb of God] and immediately follow Christ. They recognize their salvation and act on it. Such a response to the presence of Christ lies at the heart of Christian vocation and, therefore, the monastic one."

❧ What light does this image shine on your understanding of Jesus as the Lamb of God and the call to discipleship implied in that declaration?

Do you recognize the style and design of this illumination from others we have seen? What is the connection to those other passages?

This is the fourth illumination by Thomas Ingmire we've discussed. The other three were the Ten Commandments and A Poisonous Serpent in *Pentateuch*, and the Sermon on the Mount in Matthew's Gospel. All but the serpent focus on the revelation of God in and as Word. The connection between God and word has always been a favorite of scribes, some of whom spent their lives trying to convey God in words on a page. This of course has special resonance with calligraphers.

This passage significantly connects the *logos* that John introduced in his first verse ("In the beginning was the Word") and the Old Testament revelation. In fact, the phrase "I AM" used in John's Gospel is a direct reference to Exodus 3:14, "God said to Moses, 'I AM WHO I AM.' He said further, 'Thus you shall say to the Israelites, "I AM has sent me to you."'" In Hebrew, "I am who I am" is the ineffable name of the Lord God—YHWH, written without vowels to show that it cannot be uttered aloud. John the evangelist identifies Jesus with his heavenly Father every time he uses I AM in the gospel.

These sayings also connect to the Old Testament metaphors for God, which makes them even richer. Each one adds to the attributes of Christ: gate, bread, vine, light, and way. Each is a living symbol of who Christ is, deepening our understanding of the revelation.

How is this illumination built like the others, particularly the Ten Commandments? Again there are a series of vertical panels, this time five for the five metaphors of the I AM statements: the bread, the gate, the way, the light, and the true vine. (We have of course seen other fives, among them the books of the Pentateuch and the books of Psalms.) The text of the Ten Commandments dissolved down from the base of the illumination, whereas here the base is the word YHWH. The illumination rises here, sending

The I AM Sayings

JOHN 6:25-40; 8:12-20; 10:7-18; 14:6-14; 15:1-11
I am the way, and the truth, and the life. No one comes to the Father except through me. (14:6)

up geometrical sparks and spinning suns, as well as the arcs we recognize from Ingmire's illustration of the Beatitudes.

❡ What does it mean for the Son of God to say each of these sayings? What does this illumination seem to say about the kind of gate this is, about the way and where it leads, about light and wine and bread?

Which figures draw your attention in each panel? With whom do you identify?

In this illumination by Aidan Hart, with contributions from Donald Jackson and Sally Mae Joseph, we see a return to the Orthodox icon style. A comparison of what has changed in the two panels tells us all we need to know about this story.

In the first panel, one of the temple officials holds the Hebrew word for adultery out of the frame. He is literally using the Law as a weapon, a word in one hand and a stone in the other. The word extends beyond the frame to impli-cate us in the judgment, along with the direct gaze from the man stand-ing beside him, who seems to hold the stone out to us. Jesus, however, bends away from these figures, dis-tancing himself. The woman's face and hands register fear and pleading.

In the second panel, much has changed. The scene is now between Jesus and the woman, whose face and gesture register repentance and grat-itude. Beside her is a pile of stones, and there are three behind Jesus too, as though dropped by the two men who stood behind him in the first panel. In this panel the curtain that was drawn over the doorway is moved aside. Jesus raises his hand in blessing, extending an invitation to her to proceed into the gold hallway, into a world where she is commanded not to sin again. In this panel we can identify with the woman instead of with her accusers.

Woman Taken in Adultery

JOHN 7:53–8:11
Let anyone among you who is without sin be the first to throw a stone at her. (8:7b)

Raising of Lazarus

JOHN 11:1-57

When he had [prayed, Jesus] cried with a loud voice, "Lazarus, come out!" (11:43)

What moment in this dramatic story is captured by the image?

In this illumination we are inside the tomb, behind Lazarus, looking out at Christ bathed in the tunnel of light. A death-head moth spreads its patterned wings amidst the patterned wrappings of Lazarus' shroud. Lazarus is completely in darkness. The scene is a contrast between the powers of darkness and powers of light. The white light of the tunnel from which Christ is calling Lazarus forth reminds us of stories of people who describe near death experiences. The figure of Christ appears in the white light of truth, the light in which the viewer must make a decision of faith.

From this view, Christ is hardly recognizable. Lazarus too is a shadowy figure. What is most clear is the moth, the shroud, and the words of Jesus, another I AM statement, "I AM the resurrection and the life" (v. 25). These words speak to us, not just Lazarus, as Jesus asked Martha about her faith in him as Messiah, not as friend or even healer. It is this miracle that will start Jesus on the road to Jerusalem and the crucifixion, the real triumph of light over darkness, life over death. But here we stand with Lazarus poised on the edge of death and life and contemplate our own faith.

❧ Re-reading the story, can you put yourself in the place of each of the figures?

RAISING OF LAZARUS

THE ART OF THE SAINT JOHN'S BIBLE

How many elements of the Passion of Christ do you see in this illumination?

In this final illumination in John's Gospel, one of four different takes on Jesus' Passion, Crucifixion, and Resurrection, the central focus is on Mary Magdalene and Jesus' appearance to her. Again, elements from other illuminations should begin to come together for us. Here Christ is robed, as in the transfiguration, but with shades of royal purple. We stand behind him as we stood behind Lazarus, not direct witnesses of his glory but contemplating the events past, present, and future. In the background we see the same tree we saw in the illumination of Emmaus, a tie to that other resurrection story. Farther back is the tomb, flanked by two figures in white, angels in John's Gospel but elsewhere messengers of the Resurrection.

Also in the background are the three crosses of Golgotha, luminous now and tinged with gold. The stamped patterns from the carpet pages suggest this is both an end and merely a pause before the beginning. Likewise the vibrant strokes of yellow and blue take us beyond the dawn of Mary's first discovery to the fullness of day in which Christ appears and will appear again.

Like the illumination of John the Baptist at the beginning of Mark's Gospel, this one also reverses the view from conventional religious depictions of the scene. Usually it is Jesus who is highlighted, shown in some way transfigured. This time Mary is the most detailed figure on the page, fully corporeal in her decorated red garment. Her face is red, reflecting the glory she sees in Jesus' face. Instead of seeing Jesus, we see him in her response. Her hand becomes translucent, however, as she reaches to touch Jesus' face. We can see that she wants to hold on to the Jesus she knew on earth, but he tells her to embrace instead the fullness of the resurrection, the new life of Jesus ascended to the Father.

For those who read Hebrew, the word beside Mary Magdalene may look like a misspelling, "Rabbouli." Actually, the writing is the Aramaic word for rabbi, or teacher, "Rabbouni." What appears to be the Hebrew "lamed," or letter *l*,

The Resurrection

JOHN 20:1-23
Jesus said to her, "Woman, why are you weeping? Whom are you looking for?" (20:15)

THE RESURRECTION

is pronounced as *n* in Aramaic. The Committee on Illumination and Text chose the Aramaic spelling to show the connection to one of the oldest Christian churches in existence, the Syrian. The original New Testament was written in Greek, but it was translated very early into Aramaic to be used by the Syrian Church. Their translation of the Bible is the closest example we have of the language actually spoken by Jesus and his disciples.

❧ What does it mean that the gospel illuminations end with this image? How does it complete the story of Jesus' ministry and purpose?

THE ART OF THE SAINT JOHN'S BIBLE

ACTS

WHY DO YOU THINK the Committee included Acts in the same volume as the gospels? It feels right to turn the page from the gospels and enter immediately into the life of the church described in the book of Acts. John's Gospel ends with Jesus commissioning Peter to go out and "Feed my lambs" (v. 15). Matthew's Gospel also ends with the Great Commission, and in Mark's Gospel the apostles' ministry appears in both the short and long endings. The author of Luke, who also wrote Acts, ends with Jesus telling the disciples to stay in Jerusalem until they are clothed with power—which happens in Acts 2 during the feast of Pentecost. In other words, Acts picks up right where the gospels leave off.

There are thematic and artistic connections between the gospels and Acts you will want to look for in the miniatures. References to discipleship have been made throughout the gospels and occur again in this story of the founding of the church. Acts falls into two basic parts: chapters 1–12 center on the Apostle Peter, while chapters 13–28 focus on Paul. In a sense, the book is about the acts of two apostles, Peter and Paul. Peter was one of the twelve apostles with Jesus during his ministry on earth, one of the apostles present at the Transfiguration, a key figure in the Passion accounts. We have met him already at Peter's Confession, where Jesus said he would build his church on Peter.

Paul did not know Jesus, and in fact was a Pharisee who persecuted the early Christians after Jesus' death and tried to stamp out what was then a sect of Judaism. After his dramatic conversion, recounted in chapter 9, he went on to be the primary founder of Christianity among the Gentiles. His letters to various churches are the earliest pieces of writing in the New Testament. His theology was also embraced by Martin Luther in the sixteenth century, whose interpretation of Paul shaped many of the ideas of the Protestant Reformation. That theology is derived primarily from Paul's letters, however, and not from the story of his mission as recounted here in Acts.

In a way the book of Acts is a bridge between the gospels and Paul's letters. It can also be read as a parallel to Jesus' own story. Peter and Paul follow Jesus in making journeys, teaching in synagogues and on the road, and proclaiming

THE ACTS OF THE APOSTLES

In the first book, Theophilus, I wrote about all that Jesus did and taught from the beginning until the day when he was taken up to heaven, after giving instructions through the Holy Spirit to the apostles whom he had chosen. After his suffering he presented himself alive to them by many convincing proofs, appearing to them during forty days and speaking about the kingdom of God. While staying with them, he ordered them not to leave Jerusalem, but to wait there for the promise of the Father. "This," he said, "is what you have heard from me; for John baptized with water, but you will be baptized with the Holy Spirit not many days from now." So when they had come together, they asked him, "Lord, is this the time when you will restore the kingdom to Israel?" He replied, "It is not for you to know the times or periods that the Father has set by his own authority. But you will receive power when the Holy Spirit has come upon you; & you will be my witnesses in Jerusalem, in all Judea and Samaria, and to the ends of the earth." When he had said this, as they were watching, he was lifted up, and a cloud took him out of their sight. While he was going & they were gazing up toward heaven, suddenly two men in white robes stood by them. They said, "Men of Galilee, why do you stand looking up toward heaven? This Jesus, who has been taken up from you into heaven, will come in the same way as you saw him go into heaven." Then they returned to Jerusalem from the mount called Olivet, which is near Jerusalem, a sabbath day's journey away. When they had entered the city, they went to the room upstairs where they were staying, Peter, and John, and James, and Andrew, Philip and Thomas, Bartholomew and Matthew, James son of Alphaeus, and Simon the Zealot, and Judas son of James. All these were constantly devoting themselves to prayer, together with certain women, including Mary the mother of Jesus, as well as his brothers. In those days Peter stood up among the believers (together the crowd numbered about one hundred twenty persons) and said, "Friends, the scripture had to be fulfilled, which the Holy Spirit through David foretold concerning Judas, who became a guide for those who arrested Jesus—for he was numbered among us and was allotted his share in this ministry. (Now this man acquired a field with the reward of his wickedness; and falling headlong, he burst open in the middle and all his bowels gushed out. This became known to all the residents of Jerusalem, so that the field was called in their language Hakeldama, that is Field of Blood.) For it is written in the book of Psalms,

'Let his homestead become desolate,
and let there be no one to live in it';

and

'Let another take his position of overseer.'

So one of the men who have accompanied us during all the time that the Lord Jesus went in and out among us, beginning from the baptism of John until the day when he was taken up from us—one of these must become a witness with us to his resurrection." So they proposed two, Joseph called Barsabbas, who was also known as Justus, and Matthias. Then they prayed & said, "Lord, you know everyone's heart. Show us which one of these two you have chosen to take the place in this ministry and apostleship from which Judas turned aside to go to his own place." And they cast lots for them, and the lot fell on Matthias; and he was added to the eleven apostles.

2

When the day of Pentecost had come they were all together in one place. And suddenly from heaven there came a sound like the rush of a violent wind, and it filled the entire house where they were sitting. Divided tongues, as of fire, appeared among them, and a tongue rested on each of them. All of them were filled with the Holy Spirit and began to speak in other languages, as the Spirit gave them ability. Now there were devout Jews from every nation under heaven living in Jerusalem. And at this sound the crowd gathered and was bewildered, because each one heard them speaking in the native language of each. Amazed & astonished, they asked, "Are not all these who are speaking Galileans? And how is it that we hear, each of us, in our own native language? Parthians, Medes, Elamites, and residents of Mesopotamia, Judea and Cappadocia, Pontus and Asia, Phrygia and Pamphylia, Egypt and the parts of Libya belonging to Cyrene, and visitors from Rome, both Jews and proselytes, Cretans and Arabs—in our own languages we hear them speaking about God's deeds of power." All were amazed and perplexed, saying to one another, "What does this mean?" But others sneered and said, "They are filled with new wine." But Peter, standing with the eleven, raised his voice and addressed

REPENT &
BE BAPTIZED
EVERY ONE OF
YOU IN THE
NAME OF
JESUS CHRIST
SO THAT
YOUR SINS
MAY BE
FORGIVEN;
AND YOU
WILL RECEIVE
THE GIFT
OF THE
HOLY
SPIRIT:

---

salvation and God's kingdom. Before Jesus died, he promised to give his Holy Spirit, to further reveal God and build up the church. The book of Acts begins with Pentecost and the origins of the church.

In what way does this illumination make reference to both the past and present life of the church?

Pentecost

ACTS 1:6-11; 2:1-47
And suddenly from heaven there came a sound like the rush of a violent wind, and it filled the entire house where they were sitting. (2:2)

This illumination captures the event of Pentecost, when the Holy Spirit was poured out on the apostles as a fulfillment of time and history. It is the start of the Christian Church, and from this moment forward the good news will be proclaimed and peoples will be baptized in the name of Jesus Christ. As the text notes, "devout Jews from every nation under heaven" are already in Jerusalem for the great Jewish pilgrimage feast of Pentecost, fifty days after Passover (2:5). Luke's passage makes this event a fulfillment of the prophecy in Isaiah, "In days to come the mountain of the Lord's house shall be established as the highest of the mountains, and shall be raised above the hills; all the nations shall stream to it" (Isa 2:2). Just so, this illumination joins the past and present, Jerusalem and the Abbey Church in Collegeville, to show the scope of the ministry of the church.

The center of the illumination is marked by a gold column of fire and smoke. At the top of the column are the moon on the left and the sun on the right. Unnamed heavenly bodies dart about as streaks of flame pelting the earth in a visual allusion to the "tongues, as of fire" in Acts 2:3. Much of the imagery comes from the prophecy of Joel (2:28-31), describing the day of the Lord with all its traditional imagery: blood, fire, smoky mists, and heavenly portents, to which Peter refers in his speech (Acts 2:17-21). However, in this scene the Lukan author shows the Day of the Lord as hopeful, a fulfillment and building up, not as one of destruction. The hope of the passage, and of the illumination, is life in the Holy Spirit in history and eternity.

Peter's keys punctuate the call to repentance and the seal of the church. The wall of Jerusalem and the twelve apostles there give way to the rising granite edifice of Saint John's Abbey Church. At the top of the gold column is the cross as seen in the Abbey Church's prominent bell banner. Church bells are but one symbol of the good news announced to the world. Finally, the crowd at the base of the image is based on Donald Jackson's recollection of a Saint John's University football game. The checkered flags fluttering along the ground fly on the Saint John's campus on special occasions. Here at the start of the story of earliest Christianity, the illumination makes good use of the local associations to Saint John's University and Abbey.

THE ART OF THE SAINT JOHN'S BIBLE

REPENT AND
BE BAPTIZED
EVERY ONE OF
YOU
IN THE NAME OF
JESUS CHRIST

PENTECOST

Life in Community

ACTS 4:32-35
Now the whole group of those who believed were of one heart and soul, and no one claimed private ownership of any possessions. (4:32)

What does this miniature say about who makes up the community of believers?

This is a rich illumination that draws directly from Eastern Orthodox icon traditions. The idealized vision of Christ's followers in Acts 4:32-35 is here represented with idealized figures. Aidan Hart's icon painting in this collaboration with Donald Jackson gives this image of Christian unity symbolic weight. Although the passage is brief, the illumination is richly detailed and must be "read" like an icon. Like many early renaissance religious paintings, the illumination includes the pastoral imagery of a deer and various trees to tie it to the contemporary setting. These link the early church to Saint John's Abbey, along with renderings of the Abbey Church with the bell banner on the right and Stella Maris Chapel, a small chapel on the shores of a campus lake, Lake Sagatagan. The palm trees and other exotic trees are based on a painted mural in the Great Hall of Saint John's Abbey, the monk's primary place of worship until 1961.

The main part of the illumination combines elements from Eastern Orthodox icons of Pentecost, the Ascension of Christ, and the Last Supper. Pentecost icons traditionally show the twelve apostles sitting on curved benches as they are here. Additionally, there is usually the figure of an old man in the space below, where the altar is in this image. He is called "Kosmos" and holds a white cloth with twelve scrolls on it, one for each of the twelve apostles. He represents the world that the apostles are being sent out into with the good news. Various figures in this miniature hold scrolls, while others hold books, and one a small child.

At the center of the community, as in many post-resurrection icons, is the Virgin Mary, representing the Christian church. Peter sits at her right hand (holding a scroll), and it is possible that Paul is on her left. Paul often appears in Eastern Pentecost and Ascension icons, although he was not a follower of Jesus until decades later. Icons are not meant to be literal pictures of a story, but to reflect the theology of the passage. That is certainly true in this case.

LIFE IN COMMUNITY

Six apostles sit on each side, and beyond them are other saints of the church. They are meant to evoke saints throughout church history, but are not based on any specific figures. Who do you see there? They are men and women, clerics but also lay people, and as time catches up to the present, the man and woman on the end of each row are more reflective of the world church, a woman wearing a Guatemalan skirt and a man in a Middle Eastern tunic and vest.

All are gathered around the central table set with the elements of a supper or feast. This table is like the "reclining" tables of the first century, although circular to fit the design of the illumination. A fresco at the Holy Monastery of Pec in Kosovo has a scene of the Pentecost on an archway with an image of the Last Supper nested into it.

In front of the seated saints is an altar with the Holy Scriptures and the Eucharist, elements of Christianity that unite them and mark the earliest Christian liturgical practices. The altar is painted in reverse perspective, like the manger in Luke's nativity. The earliest disciples met in homes to break bread and, as is written in the top left, "gave their testimony to the resurrection of the Lord Jesus" (4:33).

Indeed, crowning the scene is Jesus Christ holding a book open to reveal his identifying name, "I AM," which connects him to God the Father (YHWH), and the Holy Spirit. The image of Christ comes from Eastern icons of the Ascension into heaven. He is framed by the Greek letters that spell Jesus Christ. Further, he is seated on rainbows, and accompanied by two angels, as in many Eastern depictions of the Ascension. The shape of the blue panel behind him is a mandorla, which we saw also in the image of the crucifixion in Luke's Gospel. The almond-shaped background is commonly used for the risen Christ in the Eastern tradition.

This complex miniature brings together three main texts in the opening of the book of Acts: the Ascension (Acts 1:6-12); Pentecost (Acts 2); and the Ideal Community (Acts 4:32-35). The description of the peaceful, united community has had a profound effect on monastic life, where members of orders strive to be "of one heart and soul" and refrain from private ownership. It is no surprise to find the cross in the margin of the text at verses 4:32 and 4:35, indicating that Saint Benedict quotes these verses in his Rule, along with the morality tale in Acts 5:1-11. Even the early church was beset by strife and conflict, disorganized and argumentative. Still, icons are images meant for meditation, not to reflect historical fact. In this image we keep before us the elements of our unity—the bread and wine and holy Word of God.

THE ART OF THE SAINT JOHN'S BIBLE

We keep in mind that we are called to community, not life alone, and work toward living according to the will of Christ and making God's way known. This work was not completed by early Christians, but continues as we add to the line of saints, who even in this image break the boundary of the circle and continue into the margins, where many of God's people are to be found.

The Life of Paul

ACTS OF THE APOSTLES
9:1-22; 15:1-35; 17:16-34;
22:17-21; 25–28
He is an instrument whom I have chosen to bring my name before Gentiles and kings and before the people of Israel. (9:15)

What details from the stories do you see in this image of Paul?

The book of Acts is dominated by two major figures: Peter and Paul. When considering a full-page illumination of Paul, the Committee on Illumination and Text decided to concentrate on Paul's life and save the development of his theology for the last volume of *The Saint John's Bible,* Letters and Revelation. Still, they wanted a composite or anthology of incidents from Paul's life, as there had been an anthology of parables in Luke. In addition to the challenge of bringing story to life as image, which Donald Jackson faced throughout the process, he was determined that this Life of Paul would stand as a unified painting, despite the extraordinary number of details about Paul mentioned in Acts.

The figure of Paul is bigger than life and has transformed history. Nowhere is this more clear than in the image of Paul holding a broken church building. The church has a strong resemblance to Saint Peter's Basilica in Rome, the city where both Peter and Paul nurtured the early Christian community and where both were martyred under the Emperor Nero. This image is not without irony, for there is evidence that these two apostles of the church did not always have an amicable relationship. Further, some have pointed to Paul's place in the Reformation; Martin Luther used Paul's writings to establish some of his most important doctrines. The Reformation literally split the church. What do you make of the fact that Paul cradles both pieces? What does it mean that he is clothed in a Jewish prayer shawl, the sign of his upbringing as a devout Jew? Do these elements work together or in tension?

What, moreover, do you make of Paul's gaze, forward, determined, yet a sideways glance? This portrait by Aidan Hart can be compared to the final image of Moses in *Pentateuch,* where his gaze captured the whole story. Some have remarked that his figure shows a combination of determination and hesitancy, as though slightly drawn back or unsure. For one who had to take so much on faith, and who

THE LIFE OF PAUL

spoke so much about faith, the combination of confidence and doubt describes a life of faith for every believer.

Paul was a man of the cities, and buildings dominate this image. The Mediterranean sailing vessel marks him as a traveler, one who took at least three sea journeys and was shipwrecked on one of them. Still, his feet are prominent, clad in sandals, and it was on foot Paul primarily took his message.

The buildings are a mix of sacred and secular, churches and walls, gates and municipal buildings. They are ancient and modern, and include a block of apartments from Fifth Avenue in New York at the top left leading to one of Marcel Breuer's dormitories at Saint John's University. On the upper right is a small image of the Stella Maris Chapel on the abbey grounds and of the cross at the abbey cemetery. At Paul's left elbow are the arches from the entrance to the Basilica of the Holy Sepulcher in Jerusalem. Also in the mix are textile patterns behind the open window, more signs of the reach of Paul's mission into human communities. The complex of arches and gates speak everywhere of his journey in and out of community, his movement forward and sometimes restriction through imprisonment, his escape through windows and over walls, as he made his way through the labyrinth of the first century Greco-Roman world.

Two pieces of text frame the image. At the top, from Paul recounting the story of his conversion: "I saw a light from heaven" (Acts 26:13). At the bottom is God's direction to Paul: "I have set you to be a light to the Gentiles, so that you may bring salvation to the ends of the earth" (Acts 13:47). Indeed, light fills the spaces of this illumination.

Why end the volume with an illumination of this verse which appears in the first chapter of Acts and again at Acts 13:47?

The final page of this volume uses only two colors, ultramarine blue and bronze, in addition to black and white. Again the image brings together the unity and chaos of creation, God's presence in heaven and on earth through his followers and their witness to the resurrection. Although the verse returns the reader to the first chapter of Acts, it is more a prophecy than a coda. At the end of the book of Acts, Paul has reached Rome, at that time the center of the civilized world. His mission to the ends of the earth is complete, and the rest is left to us. We are to bring the message of salvation to the ends of the earth, which means something quite different today.

Here the earth is shown suspended in the expanding universe, the African continent clearly defined. Donald Jackson has pointed out that this is the first hand-made Bible to feature the earth as it is actually seen from space. To the ends of the earth in biblical times meant a few thousand miles, the province of a few empires, and most people didn't travel more than a hundred miles in a lifetime. Today we apprehend both the vastness of the globe, and the smallness of it in relation to the universe, or as experienced through high-speed technologies. A comet overhead will remind some readers of Hale Bop, which was visible to the naked eye in the summer of 1997, but also perhaps of the shape of galaxies. Stencilled over the image of the dynamic universe is the cross pattern from the carpet pages. You can also see the interlocking circles of gold filigree that has been a motif throughout the volume. In fact, although another stamp was used, gold filigree was prominent in the illumination of the Loaves and Fishes, another example of God's ever-expanding reach.

◖ As you reach the end of your reflections on *Gospels and Acts,* what do you know now that you didn't before?

To the Ends of the Earth

ACTS 1:8

"But you will receive power when the Holy Spirit has come upon you; and you will be my witnesses in Jerusalem, in all Judea and Samaria, and to the ends of the earth." (1:8)

TO THE ENDS OF THE EARTH

If these short pieces have sparked your interest in icons, there are many good websites with more images of Eastern icons. There are also a number of good books on the subjects of calligraphy, iconography, & illumination, some of which are listed in a bibliography that follows.

BIBLIOGRAPHY OF SOURCES RELATED TO CALLIGRAPHY AND ILLUMINATION

Alexander, Jonathan J.G. *Medieval Illuminators and Their Methods of Work*. New Haven, CT: Yale University Press, 1994.

Backhouse, Janet. *The Illuminated Page: Ten Centuries of Manuscript Painting in The British Library*. Toronto: University of Toronto Press, 1997.

Brown, Michelle P. *Understanding Illuminated Manuscripts: A Guide to Technical Terms*. Los Angeles: Getty Trust Publications, 1994.

Calderhead, Christopher. *Illuminating the Word: The Making of The Saint John's Bible*. Collegeville, MN: Liturgical Press, 2005.

De Hamel, Christopher. *A History of Illuminated Manuscript*. London: Phaidon Press, 1997.

Drogin, Marc. *Medieval Calligraphy: Its History and Technique*. NY: Dover Publications, 1989.

Fingernagel, Andreas, and Christian Gastgeber, eds. *In the Beginning was the Word: The Power and Glory of Illuminated Bibles*. Los Angeles: Taschen, 2003.

Forest, Jim. *Praying with Icons*. Maryknoll, NY: Orbis Books, 1997.

Hendrix, Lee and Thea Vignau-Wilberg. *Nature Illuminated: Flora and Fauna from the Court of Emperor Rudolf II*. Los Angeles: Getty Trust Publications, 1997.

Kelly, Jerry and Alice Koeth, eds. *Artist & Alphabet: Twentieth Century Calligraphy and Letter Art in America*. Intro by Donald Jackson. Boston: David R. Godine Publishers, 2000.

Jackson, Donald. *Gospels and Acts*. The Saint John's Bible. Collegeville, MN: Liturgical Press, 2005.

—— *Pentateuch*. The Saint John's Bible. Collegeville, MN: Liturgical Press, 2006.

—— *Prophets*. The Saint John's Bible. Collegeville, MN: Liturgical Press, 2007.

—— *Psalms* The Saint John's Bible. Collegeville, MN: Liturgical Press, 2006.

Lovett, Patricia. *Calligraphy and Illumination: A History and Practical Guide*. NY: Harry N. Abrams, 2000.

Nes, Solrunn. *The Mystical Language of Icons*. Grand Rapids, MI: Wm. B. Eerdmans Publishing Company, 2005.

Ouspensky, Leonid. *The Meaning of Icons*. Crestwood, NY: St. Vladimirs Seminary Press, 1999.

Zibawi, Mahhoud. *The Icon: Its Meaning and History*. Collegeville, MN: Liturgical Press, 1993.

For more information on *The Saint John's Bible*, visit the websites:
http://saintjohnsbible.org or http://sjbible.org

I — n those / wilder / for the / 'This is the / when he sai / "The voice

I — n the tim / in Bethl / East ea / child who has / observed his / him hom...

H — e ma / of ac / and / three cubits high. / corners; its horns

A — grip / to sp / out / 2 "I consider n / King Agrippa, I / all the accusatic

A — s he / birth / who / he was born bli / man nor his pa / that God's wor

A — ft / an / 29 / of the Israeli / by their ances...

D — o / 2 / n / † will be the m / speck in you / log in your e

Y — ou s / shee / shall / the owner does / know who the / own house, an

T — 2 / he LOR / on ano / Israel / LORD has comn / Israel slaughters / or slaughters it o

V — "Very t / ente / in b / 2 The one who / the sheep. 3 The...

J — acob se / lived as / the story / seventeen yea

T — he LOR / of Ma / tent ir / and saw three m / saw them, he ra...

T — he tw / & Lor / Wher / and bowed dow / said, "Please, m / house and spen

T — he Lo / to th / them / all the leaders / man's name on / the staff of Lev

T — he Lo / and y / bear r / with the sanctu / shall bear respon / the priesthood,

O — ne sal / the gr / heads / and ate them. B / are you doing wh...

O — n th / ting / & c / and had anoin / all its utensils, / ancestral hou...

O — f the / mac / ister / sacred vestmen / 2 manded Moses / blue, purple, ar

T — 2 / he Lo / to the / am t / do as they do in / and you shall n / to which I am b

W — h / vited the people / the people ate / Israel yoked its

W — sound like the / the entire hous

W — 2 saying to th / and immedia / a colt with her

W — h / 2 / him & knelt bef / you can make m / & touched him.

INSECTS BY CHRIS TOMLIN:

Genesis 4–6	butterflies
Exodus 7	dragonflies
Matthew 10	dragonfly
Matthew 17	butterfly
Acts 12	butterfly
Acts 20	moth

CORRECTION BIRDS:

Genesis 30

Exodus 38

Leviticus 19

Mark 3

MARGINALIA:

Genesis 8	The Flood
Genesis 50	Menorah
Leviticus 17	Decorative border
Deuteronomy 34	Menorah
Mark 2	monk reading
Matthew 14	mandala / arabesque
Mark 11	"Listen to Him"
Mark 16:9-20	Additional bookplates & decoration in margin

GENESIS 4

MARK 2

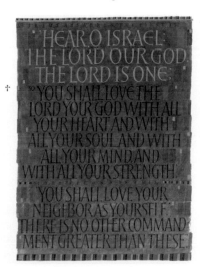

MARK 12:29-31

Index of Text Treatments

Leviticus 19:2   You shall be holy, for I the Lord your God am holy.

Leviticus 19:18   You shall not take vengeance or bear a grudge against any of your people, but you shall love your neighbor as yourself: I am the Lord.

Leviticus 19:34   The alien who resides with you shall be to you as the citizen among you; you shall love the alien as yourself, for you were aliens in the land of Egypt: I am the Lord your God.

Numbers 6:24-26   The Lord bless you and keep you; the Lord make his face to shine upon you, and be gracious to you; the Lord lift up his countenance upon you, and give you peace.

Numbers 20:12   But the Lord said to Moses and Aaron, "Because you did not trust in me, to show my holiness before the eyes of the Israelites, therefore you shall not bring this assembly into the land that I have given them."

Deuteronomy 6:4-5   Hear O Israel: The Lord is our God, the Lord alone. You shall love the Lord your God with all your heart, and with all your soul, and with all your might.

Deuteronomy 30:19-20 I call heaven and earth to witness against you today that I have set before you life and death, blessings and curses. Choose life so that you and your descendants may live, loving the Lord your God, obeying him, and holding fast to him; for that means life to you and length of days, so that you may live in the land that the Lord swore to give to your ancestors, to Abraham, to Isaac, and to Jacob.

Psalm 1   Happy are those
                        who do not follow the advice of the wicked,
                        or take the path that sinners tread,
                        or sit in the seat of scoffers;
                        but their delight is in the law of the Lord,
                        and on his law they meditate day and night . . .

THE ART OF THE SAINT JOHN'S BIBLE

Luke 2:14	"Glory to God in the highest heaven, and on earth peace among those whom he favors!"
Luke 2:28-32 *Canticle of* *Simeon*	"Master, now you are dismissing your servant in peace, according to your word; for my eyes have seen your salvation, which you have prepared in the presence of all peoples, a light for revelation to the Gentiles and for glory to your people Israel."
Luke 10:27	"You shall love the Lord your God with all your heart, and with all your soul, and with all your strength, and with all your mind; and your neighbor as yourself."
Luke 23:46	"Father, into your hands I commend my spirit."

OTHER PSALM TREATMENTS

Psalm 6	O Lord, do not rebuke me in your anger or discipline me in your wrath.
Psalm 32	Happy are those whose transgression is forgiven, whose sin is covered.
Psalm 38	O Lord, do not rebuke me in your anger, or discipline me in your wrath.
Psalm 51	Have mercy on me O God, according to your steadfast love; according to your abundant mercy blot out my transgression.
Psalm 102	Hear my prayer, O Lord; let my cry come to you.
Psalm 130	Out of the depths I cry to you, O Lord.
Psalm 143	Hear my prayer, O Lord; give ear to my supplications in your faithfulness; answer me in your righteousness.

THE ART OF THE SAINT JOHN'S BIBLE

Index of Artists

ILLUMINATORS

Donald Jackson (Artistic Director and Illuminator — Monmouthshire, Wales)

One of the world's leading calligraphers, Donald Jackson is the artistic director and illuminator of *The Saint John's Bible*. From his scriptorium in Wales, he oversees scribes, artists, and craftsmen who work with him on the handwriting and illumination of this seven-volume, 1,150-page book. His studio/workshop is the only calligraphy atelier in the United Kingdom where artist calligraphers are still regularly employed as assistants, maintaining the highest traditions of this ancient art in a modern context.

From an early age, Jackson sought to combine the use of the ancient techniques of the calligrapher's art with the imagery and spontaneous letter forms of his own time. As a teenager, his first ambition was to be "The Queen's Scribe" and a close second was to inscribe and illuminate the Bible. His talents were soon recognized and his ambitions fulfilled.

At the age of twenty, while still a student himself, Jackson was appointed a visiting lecturer (professor) at the Camberwell College of Art, London. Within six years, he became the youngest artist calligrapher chosen to take part in the Victoria and Albert Museum's first International Calligraphy Show after the war and appointed a scribe to the Crown Office at the House of Lords. As a scribe to Her Majesty Queen Elizabeth II, he was responsible for the creation of official state documents. In conjunction with a wide range of other calligraphic projects, he executed Historic Royal documents under The Great Seal and Royal Charters. In 1985, he was decorated by the Queen with the Medal of The Royal Victorian Order (MVO) which is awarded for personal services to the Sovereign.

Jackson is an elected Fellow and past Chairman of the prestigious Society of Scribes and Illuminators, and in 1997, was named Master of 600-year-old Guild of Scriveners of the city of London. His personally innovative work and inspirational teaching, together with books, a film series, and exhibitions in Europe, North America, Puerto Rico, Australia, and China, have led to his being widely acknowledged as a seminal influence on the growth of Western calligraphy over the past 25 years. In 1980, he wrote *The Story of Writing,* which has since been published in many editions and seven languages. His thirty-year retrospective exhibition, *Painting With Words,* premiered at the Minneapolis Institute of Arts in Minneapolis, Minnesota in August 1988 and traveled to thirteen museums and galleries.

Since the time of his first lectures in New York and Puerto Rico (1968), Donald Jackson has had a very stimulating influence on the growth of modern Western calligraphy in the United States through the many workshops and lectures he has given. It was the first of the International Assembly of Lettering Artists seminars, inspired by Jackson, which brought him to Saint John's Abbey and University for the first time in 1981. He has since attended and lectured at several other of these annual Assemblies including those held at Saint John's in 1984 and 1990. Jackson returned again to Saint John's in the summer of 1996 to serve as one of the keynote speakers at *Servi Textus: The Servants of the Text,* a symposium which included a calligraphy exhibition featuring Jackson's work along with that of other artists, many of whom were his past students and past associates of his atelier.

Interpretive illuminations, incipits, and special treatments in these volumes are the work of Donald Jackson, unless otherwise noted below.

Hazel Dolby (Illuminator — Hampshire, England)

Trained at Camberwell Art College, London, and later at the Roehampton Institute with Ann Camp. She is a Fellow of the Society of Scribes and Illuminators (FSSI). She is a lecturer at University of Roehampton, teaching art and drawn and painted lettering, and teaches workshops in Europe and the United States. Her work is in various collections including the Poole Museum and The Crafts Study Centre, London.

Deuteronomy 6:4-5	"Hear O Israel"
Matthew 22	"You shall love the Lord"
Mark 12	"Hear O Israel"
Luke 2	"Master now you are"
Luke 10	"You shall love the Lord"

Aidan Hart (Iconographer — Shropshire, Wales)

Studied in New Zealand, the United Kingdom and Greece. He was a full-time sculptor in New Zealand before returning to the United Kingdom in 1983. Since then he has worked as a full-time iconographer. A member of the Orthodox Church, his work is primarily panel icons but also includes church frescoes, illuminations on vellum, and carved work in stone and wood. His work is in collections in over fifteen countries of the world. He has contributed to numerous publications. Visiting tutor at The Prince's School of Traditional Arts, London.

Deuteronomy 33	Death of Moses	*collaboration with Donald Jackson*
Mark 1	Decoration	
Mark 9	Transfiguration	*collaboration with Donald Jackson*
Luke 15	Anthology	*contributions to image by Donald Jackson*
John 8	Woman taken in adultery	*with contributions from Donald Jackson and Sally Mae Joseph*
Acts 4	Life in community	*collaboration with Donald Jackson*

Thomas Ingmire (Illuminator — San Francisco, California)

Trained as a landscape architect at Ohio State University and University of California, Berkeley, before beginning the study of calligraphy and medieval painting techniques in the early seventies. He is the first foreign member to be elected Fellow of the Society of Scribes and Illuminators (FSSI) (1977). Ingmire teaches throughout the United States, Canada, Australia, Europe, Japan, and Hong Kong. He has exhibited widely in the United States. His work is in many public and private collections throughout the world including San Francisco Public Library's Special Collections, The Newberry Library, Chicago, and the Victoria and Albert Museum, London.

Exodus 20	Ten Commandments
Numbers 20:12	"You did not trust"
Numbers 21:8	A Poisonous Serpent
Matthew 5	Sermon on the Mount
John 6	The "I AM" sayings

Andrew Jamieson (Illuminator — Somerset, England)

Trained at Reigate School of Art and Design, specializing in heraldry and calligraphy and manuscript illumination. He works as a heraldic artist and illustrator. His work is in public and private collections in Europe and the United States.

Matthew 14	Middle Eastern Arabesque	
Acts 27	"To the ends of the earth"	*contribution to image by Donald Jackson*
Acts 28	"You will be my witness"	*contribution to image by Donald Jackson*

Sally Mae Joseph (Scribe/Illuminator and Senior Artistic Consultant — Monmouthshire, Wales)

Studied illumination, calligraphy, and heraldry at Reigate School of Art and Design and calligraphy, applied lettering, and bookbinding at the Roehampton Institute, London. Fellow of the Society of Scribes and Illuminators (FSSI). She has exhibited and lectured in Europe and the United States. She has contributed articles to numerous publications. She was a lecturer at Roehampton Institute 1991–1993. Her work is in many public and private collections.

Genesis 50	Carpet page	
Leviticus 19:2	"You shall be holy"	
Leviticus 19:18	"You shall not take vengeance"	
Leviticus 19:34	"The alien who resides"	
Deuteronomy 33	Death of Moses	*contribution to piece by Donald Jackson in collaboration with Aidan Hart*
Deuteronomy 34	Menorah decoration	
Psalm 150	"Praise the Lord"	
Matthew 1	Decoration facing frontispiece	*contributions to piece by Donald Jackson*
Matthew 28	Carpet page	
Mark 3	Sower and the Seed	*contribution*
Mark 5	Two Cures	*contribution*
Mark 11	"Listen to Him"	
Mark 16	Carpet page	
Luke 1	Magnificat	
Luke 2	Glory to God	
Luke 15	Anthology	*contribution*
Luke 24	Decoration	
Luke 24	Carpet page—tree of life	
John 21	Decoration	
John 21	Carpet page	
Acts 2	Decoration	
Acts 27	"To the ends of the earth"	*contribution*

* writing of *Psalms* Book I (Psalms 1–41) and Book V (Psalms 107–150)
also raised and burnished gilding throughout *Psalms*
scribe for *Pentateuch*, *Psalms*, and *Gospels and Acts*

Suzanne Moore (Illuminator — Vashon Island, WA)

Earned a BFA in printmaking and drawing at the University of Wisconsin at Eau Claire, followed by the study of lettering and book design. She began creating manuscript books in the early 1980s, and melds traditional scribal techniques with contemporary aesthetics in her book work. Suzanne has taught and exhibited widely, and her books have been acquired for private and public collections in the United States and Europe, including the Pierpont Morgan Library, The Library of Congress, and The James S. Copley Library, La Jolla, California.

Numbers 6:24	"The Lord Bless You"
Deuteronomy 30:19-20	"Choose Life"
Matthew 9	Calming of the Storm
Matthew 24	Last Judgment

Chris Tomlin (Natural History Illustrator — London, England)

Trained at the Royal College of Art, London, studying natural history illustration. He has worked for Oxford University Press and the National Trust, as well as other publishers. He also studies flora and fauna in the field on expeditions as far from home as Minnesota and Madagascar, where he has worked in the rainforest recording endangered species.

Genesis 2	Garden of Eden	*contributions to piece by Donald Jackson*
Genesis 3	Adam & Eve	*contributions to piece by Donald Jackson*
Genesis 4–6	butterflies	
Genesis 29	Jacob's Ladder	*collaboration with Donald Jackson*
Genesis 34	Jacob's Dream	*contributions to piece by Donald Jackson*
Exodus 7	dragonflies	
Matthew 10	dragonfly	
Matthew 17	butterfly	
Acts 12	butterfly	
Acts 20	moth	

THE ART OF THE SAINT JOHN'S BIBLE

SCRIBES

Sue Hufton (London, England)

Trained at the Roehampton Institute, London, studying calligraphy and bookbinding. Fellow of the Society of Scribes and Illuminators (FSSI). Lecturer at the University of Roehampton, teaching calligraphy and bookbinding. Teaches in Europe, Canada, and Australia, and has led calligraphic retreats to Holy Island (Lindisfarne), United Kingdom. Editor of the SSI Journal *The Scribe* and has contributed articles to other publications.

> *Pentateuch, Gospels and Acts,* and all running heads

Donald Jackson (see biography above)

> *Pentateuch, Gospels and Acts, Psalms* Book III (73–89) and Book IV (90–106)

Sally Mae Joseph (see biography above)

> *Pentateuch, Gospels and Acts, Psalms* Book II (42–72) and Book V (107–150)

Izzy Pludwinski (Jerusalem, Israel)

Started out as a certified religious scribe (*Sofer* STaM) and branched out to calligraphy and design. He studied at the Roehampton Institute, where he completed the certificate in Calligraphy and Design. He has taught in both London and Israel.

> Hebrew running heads in *Pentateuch*

Izzy Pludwinski and Donald Jackson did the Hebrew lettering, which is extensively found in *Pentateuch*. Christopher Calderhead supplied some of the Hebrew text on the notes.

Brian Simpson (Leicestershire, England)

Studied calligraphy and heraldry (a fellow student of Donald Jackson) at Central School for Arts and Crafts, London, with Irene Wellington and Mervyn Oliver. He worked as a lettering artist and graphic designer for forty-nine years. Now he concentrates on calligraphy and heraldic art.

> *Pentateuch, Gospels and Acts, Psalms* Book I (1–41), and all chapter numbers and Psalm numbers

Michael Patella, OSB

Michael Patella, OSB, is the chair of The Saint John's Bible Committee on Illumination and Text. He is an associate professor of New Testament and teaches in both the theology department and the School of Theology at Saint John's University, where he serves as the director of the School of Theology's Early Christian World Program. He has published in the areas of Luke, Mark, and Paul, and he also writes the "Seers' Corner" for *The Bible Today*. He earned a License in Sacred Scripture from Rome's Pontifical Biblical Institute and a Doctorate in Sacred Scripture from the École biblique et archéologique francaise in Jerusalem.

Susan Wood, SCL

Susan Wood, SCL, is a professor of Theology at Marquette University, Milwaukee, Wisconsin. She taught in both the theology department and School of Theology at Saint John's University for twelve years and was the associate dean of the School of Theology for five years. She earned her bachelor's degree at Saint Mary College in Leavenworth, Kansas, her master's degree at Middlebury College, Middlebury, Vermont, and her doctorate degree at Marquette University, Milwaukee, Wisconsin.

Columba Stewart, OSB

Columba Stewart, OSB, is the executive director of the Hill Museum and Manuscript Library (HMML), the home of *The Saint John's Bible,* where he has developed HMML's projects of manuscript digitization in the Middle East. Having served on the CIT and as curator of special collections before becoming director of HMML, he often speaks about how *The Saint John's Bible* expresses the vision for the book arts and religious culture at Saint John's University. Father Columba has published extensively on monastic topics and is a professor of Monastic Studies at Saint John's School of Theology. He received his A.B. in History and Literature from Harvard College, an M.A. in Religious Studies from Yale University, and his D. Phil. in Theology from the University of Oxford.

Irene Nowell, OSB

Irene Nowell, OSB, is a Benedictine from Mount St. Scholastica in Atchison, Kansas, where she is the director of junior sisters. She is an adjunct professor of Scripture for the School of Theology at Saint John's University. Sister Irene received her bachelor's degree in music from Mt. St. Scholastica College in Kansas, master's degrees in German and Theology from The Catholic University of America and Saint John's University. She holds a Ph.D. in Biblical Studies from The Catholic University of America.

Johanna Becker, OSB

A Benedictine potter, teacher, art historian and Orientalist, Johanna Becker, OSB, combines these in the different facets of her work. As a teacher in the art department of the College of Saint Benedict and Saint John's University, she taught both studio classes (primarily ceramics) and art history focusing for the past several years on the arts of Asia. As a specialist in Asian ceramics, particularly those of seventeenth-century Japan, she has done connoisseurship for public and private museums, published a book, *Karatsu Ware* and written and lectured worldwide. Her art history classes benefit from the years she lived in Japan and her time spent in the majority of Asian countries as an art researcher. Sister Johanna holds a Bachelor of Fine Arts degree from the University of Colorado, a Master of Fine Arts degree in studio art from Ohio State University and a doctorate degree in art history from the University of Michigan. Although retired, she continues to teach Asian art history classes. She is a member of the Monastery of Saint Benedict, St. Joseph, Minnesota.

Nathanael Hauser, OSB

Nathanael Hauser, OSB, is an artist who works in egg tempera, enamel, calligraphy, and mosaic. While teaching art history as an associate professor at Saint John's University, he also taught calligraphy and the theology and practice of icon painting. Father Nathanael has undertaken commissions for churches, monastic communities, and private collections, creating icons, enameled crosses, calligraphy books, reliquaries, and Christmas crèches. His work and papers have been exhibited and presented in the United States and Rome, Italy. Father Nathanael received his bachelor's degree in Philosophy from St. John's Seminary College in Camarillo, California. He received his S.T.B. from the Pontificio Ateneo di Sant'Anselmo, Rome, and his Ph.D. in Classical and Medieval Art and Archeology from the University of Minnesota.

Alan Reed, OSB

Alan Reed, OSB, is the curator of art collections at the Hill Museum and Manuscript Library. Previously Brother Alan taught design and drawing in the joint Art Department of Saint John's University and the College of St. Benedict for twenty-five years and toward the end of that time, was chair of the department for six years. He has a Bachelor of Arts degree from Saint John's University in studio art, a Master of Art Education from the Rhode Island School of Design, and a Master of Fine Art from the University of Chicago in studio art and art theory.

Ellen Joyce

Ellen Joyce teaches Medieval History at Beloit College in Beloit, Wisconsin. Her research interests are in the role of visions and dreams in medieval monastic culture. She also has a passion for the study of illuminated manuscripts and their production and often teaches courses on topics related to books and their readers in the Middle Ages. She served on the CIT while she was employed at the Hill Museum and Manuscript Library and teaching at Saint John's University. Dr. Joyce received her master's and doctoral degrees from the Centre for Medieval Studies at the University of Toronto and her undergraduate degree in Humanities from Yale University.

Rosanne Keller

Rosanne Keller is a sculptor whose work is on permanent display throughout the United States and the United Kingdom. In 1993 she was commissioned to create a ceramic Buddha and eight ritual vessels for the private meditation room of His Holiness, the Dalai Lama. Her sculpture can be seen at St. Deiniol's Library and St. Bueno's Jesuit Retreat Center in Wales; Saint John's University and the St. Cloud Children's Home in Minnesota; Exeter Cathedral; Taize, France; and on the campus of Texas Woman's University. She has published a book on pilgrimage, *Pilgrim in Time*, and a novel, *A Summer All Her Own*, as well as texts for literacy programs.

Other members of the broader Saint John's community, including Susan Brix, Jerome Tupa, OSB, and David Cotter, OSB, have served at various times on the Committee on Illumination and Text.